The Headway Readers

President
M. Blouke Carus

**Publisher and
General Manager**
Howard R. Webber

Managing Editor
Patty Green

Art Director
Todd Sanders

**Curriculum Development
Assistant**
Diane M. Sikora

The Place Called Morning

The Headway Program
Level F

Editors
Marianne Carus
Thomas G. Anderson
Howard R. Webber

Language Arts Curriculum Development Center
Dale E. Howard, Director
Catherine E. Anderson, Associate

Open Court   La Salle, Illinois

ACKNOWLEDGMENTS:

FOR PERMISSION to reprint copyrighted material, grateful acknowledgment is made to the following publishers and persons:

Crown Publishers, Inc., for "The Umbrella" from *A Treasury of Jewish Folklore* edited by Nathan Ausubel, copyright 1948 by Crown Publishers, Inc.

The Dial Press for an adaptation of *Mandy's Grandmother* by Liesel Moak Skorpen, copyrighted © 1975 by Liesel Moak Skorpen, as it appeared in *Cricket*, September 1975.

E. P. Dutton & Co., Inc., and A. B. P. International for Chapter II from *Winnie-The-Pooh* by A. A. Milne. Illustrated by E. H. Shepard. Copyright 1926, by E. P. Dutton & Co., Inc. Renewal 1954, by A. A. Milne. Reprinted by permission of the publishers.

Follett Publishing Company, a division of Follett Corporation, for "The Great Minu" abridged from *The Great Minu* as retold by Beth P. Wilson, copyright © 1974 by Beth P. Wilson.

Funk & Wagnalls Company for "Love Like Salt," reprinted from *The Soup Stone: The Magic of Familiar Things* by Maria Leach.

Grosset & Dunlap, Inc., for "The Lady with the Lamp" from *The Story of Florence Nightingale* by Margaret Leighton. Copyright © 1952 by Margaret Leighton.

Harper & Row, Publishers, for "Alexander and His Horse" from *History Stories of Our Lands* from the volume *Tales From Far and Near,* edited by Arthur Guy Terry; and for "Narcissa" from *Bronzeville Boys and Girls* by Gwendolyn Brooks. Copyright 1956 by Gwendolyn Brooks Blakely.

Harper & Row, Publishers, Inc., for "Boa Constrictor," from *Where the Sidewalk Ends* by Shel Silverstein, copyright © 1974 by Shel Silverstein.

Holt, Rinehart and Winston, Inc., for "Stopping by Woods on a Snowy Evening," from *You Come Too* by Robert Frost. Copyright 1923, by Holt, Rinehart and Winston, Inc. Copyright renewed 1951 by Robert Frost.

Parents' Magazine Press for *The Dead Tree* by Alvin Tresselt, text copyright © 1972 by Alvin Tresselt.

Time-Life Picture Agency © Time Inc. for Margaret Bourke-White photographs on pages 177, 179, 180, and 181.

All possible care has been taken to trace ownership and obtain permission for each selection included. If any errors or omissions have occurred, they will be corrected in subsequent editions, provided they are brought to the publisher's attention.

Contents

Part One: Stories and Poems Everyone Likes

Part Two: Famous People

Part Three: Science and Nature

Part Four: For Readers Brave and Bold

ILLUSTRATORS:
Enrico Arno (5, 13, 26), Melanie Arwin (100, 148-150), Joseph Cellini (94, 103, 109, 110, 162, 166, 169), David Cunningham (133, 135), JoAnn Daley (117), Mike Eagle (81, 89-91), Hal Frenck (35, 72), Imero Gobatto (32, 39, 41, 42, 154, 156, 159), Lee Hill (6-9), Trina Schart Hyman (3, 15, 17, 19, 21, 22, 48, 50, 54), Bill Jacobson (68, 113), Robin Jacques (45), Randy Jones (65, 136), Diana Magnuson (141), Dick Martin (84), Victor Mays (98, 124), Charles McBarron (77), Barbara McClintock (79), Barbara Pritzen (cover), E. H. Shepard (58, 61, 63, 64), Krystyna Stasiak (29, 31, 151), Lorna Tomei (119), Wally Tripp (70), Mary Winifred Walter (120).

PHOTOGRAPHY:
Bettman Archives, Inc. (87), Margaret Bourke-White (177, 179, 180, 181, 182, 183), Culver Pictures (130).

DESIGN:
John Grandits, James Buddenbaum

Part One

Stories and Poems Everyone Likes

The Lion in His Den

Aesop

In the forest many years ago there lived an old lion. This lion was so old that he could no longer run and catch little animals for his food. He knew that the only way to get enough to eat was to make the other animals come to him.

So he crawled into his den and made believe that he was sick. He groaned and groaned. The little animals would hear the groans. They felt sorry for the old lion, and they would go in the den to see if they could help him. Then the lion would snap them up for his food. In this way many animals lost their lives.

One day a fox was passing by the lion's den and he heard the lion groan. The fox did not go into the den, but he stood in the entrance and said, "What's the matter, my friend?"

"Oh, I am very sick," replied the lion. "I will not live very long now. Come into my den so that I can say good-bye to you."

When the fox heard these words, he replied, "Please pardon me, friend lion, but I do not think I will come in. I see many paw prints pointing into your den, but I don't see any pointing out."

QUESTIONS

1. What trick did the old lion use to get his food?
2. Did he catch many animals by this trick?
3. Why didn't he catch the fox with his trick?
4. What is the point of this fable?

THE DEER

Old Fable

One time a deer came up to the edge of a river to get a drink. He saw himself in the water, and he was very pleased to see how large and broad his antlers were. But then he saw his legs reflected in the water, and he said to himself, "How thin and ugly my legs are!"

Suddenly a lion jumped out of the bushes and ran after the deer. The deer started to run across the open field. He was nearly out of sight of the lion when his antlers became tangled in a tree branch. The lion almost caught him. But the deer got his antlers untangled just in time. After he had run a safe distance from the lion, he said to himself, "How stupid I am! I thought that my legs were thin and ugly, and yet they have saved me. I was glad that my antlers were big and broad, but because of them I almost lost my life!"

Across the ocean and far away, a poor African farmer prepared to journey to the big city of Accra, in Ghana. He walked around his small farm, taking note of the yams and corn growing in the garden. Then he fed his chickens and goats, latched his thatched-roof hut, and started down the narrow, dusty road.

All morning and all afternoon the farmer trudged down the road, stopping only at midday for a bite to eat and a short rest. At last he reached the farms on the outskirts of the city. There he noticed a great herd of cows. Who could own such a great herd, he wondered. Seeing a man with them, he asked, "To whom do these cows belong?" The man did not know the

THE GREAT MINU

Retold by
Beth P. Wilson

language of the farmer, who had traveled so far, so he shrugged his shoulders and said, "Minu," meaning "I do not understand." The traveler thought Minu must be a person and exclaimed, "Mr. Minu must be very rich!"

Entering the city, the traveler saw some large new buildings in the town square. He wondered who might own these buildings. But the man he asked could not understand his question, so he also answered, "Minu."

"Good heavens!" cried the traveler. "What a

rich fellow Mr. Minu must be to own all those cows and these large new buildings, too!"

Soon he came to a grand hotel surrounded by beautiful grounds and mahogany trees. A group of fashionably dressed African ladies came down the front steps of the hotel. The traveler stepped up to them and asked who might be the owner of such a grand hotel. The ladies smiled and said softly, "Minu." "How wealthy Mr. Minu is!" exclaimed the astonished traveler.

He wandered from one neighborhood to another and finally came to the harbor where he saw men loading bananas, cocoa beans, and mahogany onto a fine big ship. With the blue sky above, the foamy green ocean below, and the sailors rushing about on board ship, it was an impressive sight. The traveler inquired of a bystander, "To whom does this fine big ship belong?" "Minu," replied the puzzled man who couldn't understand a word of the question. The traveler gasped. "To the great Minu also? He is the richest man I ever heard of!"

Just as the traveler was setting out for home, he saw men carrying a coffin down the main street of Accra. A long procession of people, all dressed in black, followed the men. People on the sidelines shook their heads slowly. Sad faces looked up now and then. When the traveler asked one of the mourners the name of the dead person, he received the usual reply, "Minu."

"Mr. Minu is dead?" wailed the traveler. "Poor Mr. Minu! So he had to leave all his wealth—his great herd of cows, his large new buildings and grand hotel, and his fine big ship—and die just like a poor person. Well, well, in the future I'll be content with my little hut, on my little farm, in my little village."

The long, dusty road back didn't seem as long as it had before. When the farmer arrived home, he unlatched the door of his hut and looked around inside. Then he climbed into his own snug bed and dreamed of the good foo-foo he would eat the next day.

QUESTIONS

1. Who is Mr. Minu?
2. What did the farmer learn from his trip to Accra?
3. Find the city of Accra, and the country of Ghana, on a map of Africa.
4. If somebody asks you what "foo-foo" is, what is your answer?

My Shadow
Robert Louis Stevenson

I have a little shadow that goes in and out
   with me,
And what can be the use of him is more than
   I can see.
He is very, very like me from the heels up to
   the head;
And I see him jump before me, when I jump
   into my bed.

The funniest thing about him is the way he
   likes to grow—
Not at all like proper children, which is always
   very slow;
For he sometimes shoots up taller like an
   India-rubber ball,
And he sometimes gets so little that there's
   none of him at all.

One morning, very early, before the sun was up,
I rose and found the shining dew on every
   buttercup;
But my lazy little shadow, like an arrant sleepy-
   head,
Had stayed at home behind me and was fast
   asleep in bed.

The Boy Who Cried Wolf

Aesop

Once there was a shepherd boy who took care of his sheep on a lonely hillside in the country. He had no one to talk to, and he was very lonely. One day the boy thought of a way to find some excitement. He ran down the hill and shouted, "A wolf! A wolf!"

The farmers who were working in the nearby fields heard the shouts. They thought that a wolf was eating up the boy's sheep, so they stopped their work and ran to help him.

But when they got to the hillside, the boy laughed and said, "I was only playing a joke." The farmers did not think that the boy's joke was very funny, and they were angry with him.

A few days later the boy did the same thing again. "A wolf! A wolf!" he cried. Again the farmers dropped their tools and ran to help him. But when they saw that the boy had fooled them a second time, they were very angry.

Then on the very next day a wolf did come.

"Wolf! Wolf!" cried the boy. But this time the farmers did not believe him. They went on with their work, and the wolf ate up many of the boy's sheep. The boy was very sad, but he had learned a hard lesson: If you are a liar, no one will believe you, even when you are telling the truth.

QUESTIONS

1. Why did the boy cry "Wolf" the first time?
2. Why didn't the farmers think the boy's joke was a good one?
3. Why didn't the farmers come the last time the boy cried "Wolf"?
4. What lesson did the boy learn?

MANDY'S GRAND-MOTHER

Liesel Moak Skorpen

Mandy's grandmother was coming for a visit. Mandy's mother was cleaning the house. Even the closets and the drawers.

"Will my grandmother peek in our drawers?" Mandy asked.

"Of course she won't," her mother said. "I'm just in a mood for cleaning drawers. You wouldn't understand."

WORDS TO WATCH

entertain	fumbling	scurvy
precious	formula	casting on

"I don't," said Mandy.

"How will I manage?" said Mandy's mother later. "What with the baby teething and all?"

Mandy was helping her mother make the guest room bed. "That's a bad baby," she said. "All he does is cry."

"It isn't his fault," replied her mother. "You cried too when you were cutting teeth."

"I doubt it," Mandy said.

Mandy's mother smoothed the spread. She was in a hurry. She was always in a hurry now. "You'll have to help me entertain your grandmother," she said.

"I don't know how to entertain," said Mandy.

Mandy had a picture book with a grandmother in the story. That grandmother took the little girl for walks and to the zoo. She had plenty of time to hold the girl on her lap. Mandy looked at all the pictures carefully, especially the ones with the girl on the grandmother's lap. Sometimes she liked to sit on somebody's lap. Sometimes she didn't, but sometimes she really did.

On the day that her grandmother was coming, Mandy had to pick up her room, take a bath, and change her clothes. "Do I have to take down my fort?" Mandy asked.

"Oh, I suppose not," said Mandy's mother, hurrying.

Mandy put on clean jeans and her favorite sweater and her floppy old, sloppy old hat.

"Couldn't you put on a dress?" asked her mother, holding the crying baby.

"My grandmother will like my hat," said Mandy.

Mandy's grandmother came in a furry coat and a funny

hat with flowers. She had two interesting boxes in her arms. Mandy's mother brought the baby down. He was crying again. "Isn't he precious?" her grandmother said. "And who is this little fellow?" she said to Mandy.

"Why, that's our Mandy," said Mandy's mother quickly.

"Oh, dear," said Mandy's grandmother, fumbling with her packages and trying to smile.

In the baby's box were a soft toy horse, some silly-looking suits, and a fat yellow puff that Mandy liked and wanted for herself. "I can hardly wait to see Mandy in hers," Mandy's grandmother said.

"Maybe it's cowboy clothes," Mandy thought, tearing the ribbons off her box. The dress was yellow. So was the hat. The purse had a little lace hanky inside. "Thank you," said Mandy softly but politely. She tried to smile, but it came out crooked.

The next day it rained. Mandy looked out of the kitchen window. "Yuck," she said. Mandy had the same breakfast every day: a peanut butter and banana sandwich, and tea with honey but mostly milk. "That's not a healthy breakfast," Mandy's grandmother said. "I'll fix you some oatmeal and some eggs."

"Yuck," said Mandy. "I hate eggs."

Mandy's mother was making formula. The baby was crying in his chair. Formula stuff was spread all over the kitchen. "Do me a favor, honey," said her mother. "Go in and talk to Grandmother a while." Mandy went in the living room.

"Show me your dolls," said Grandmother brightly. "How your mother used to love her dolls."

"I don't have dolls," said Mandy. "I don't like them. I have a frog, though," she said hopefully. "His name is Wart." She lifted her hat, and there was Wart sleeping on her

head. Mandy's grandmother screamed, her mother came running, and Mandy was sent outside.

"What I know about grandmothers," Mandy said to Wart, "is that they're very boring." Mandy was mad at everyone, even Wart. Wart hopped on the pirate ship she had built for them. "Not today, you scurvy toad," said Mandy.

Mandy's grandmother took a walk by herself down to the mailboxes and back. She walked in the wet garden, frowning at the weeds. She sat on the porch writing letters.

The next day Mandy's grandmother didn't come down.

"Take her up this cup of tea," Mandy's mother said.

"She doesn't like me," Mandy said.

"Of course she does," said her mother sternly. "She loves you."

Mandy knocked.

"Come in," said Mandy's grandmother softly. She was sitting by the window. Her eyes were closed.

Mandy set the tea on the table. She was thinking about the picture book, because she was feeling like sitting on somebody's lap. "I brought some tea," she said.

"Thank you, dear," Mandy's grandmother said, "but I'm not feeling very well."

Mandy saw that her grandmother had been crying. It made her stomach feel queer to think about grown-ups crying. "Tea's very good for you," she said. "It warms you up."

Mandy's grandmother closed her eyes again. She didn't take the tea.

"I think you must be very sad," said Mandy.

"I am a little sad," Mandy's grandmother said. "I was thinking about when your mother was little like you. I used to like to hold her on my lap."

"I like laps, too," said Mandy quickly. "I like laps a lot."

Mandy's grandmother held out her arms, and there was Mandy on her lap. Mandy's arms were around her neck, and Mandy's face was pressed against her shoulder.

"Are you crying?" Mandy's grandmother asked.

"No," said Mandy, crying.

They had their breakfast together by the window. Mandy had a sandwich. Mandy's grandmother had scrambled eggs and toast. They both had tea with honey and mostly milk.

After breakfast Mandy showed her grandmother the barn. She showed her the chickens and the goats and introduced her to Strawberry Pony.

"Does he bite?" her grandmother asked.

"Not if he likes you," Mandy said.

Mandy's grandmother fed him carrot sticks, and Strawberry licked her hand.

"Would you like to ride him?" Mandy asked. "Sometimes he bucks a little bit."

Mandy's grandmother thought that she wouldn't. "Hip Hip Harray!" she shouted as Mandy and Strawberry came galloping down the lane.

Mandy showed her the pirate ship. Her grandmother took a good look at Wart, but she didn't want to hold him.

"Friends don't have to share everything," she said.

Mandy thought that over and decided she was right. She showed her grandmother the secret blackberry bush. "Promise you'll never tell," she said. Her grandmother crossed her heart. They packed a lunch and ate it on the picnic rock halfway up the hill.

The next day was wet again. They talked a lot. Mandy's grandmother told her stories of when her mother was a little girl. About how she made cookies once with salt instead of

sugar, and how she used to write poems for Grandfather's birthday, and how she fell in her uncle's pond with her Easter bonnet on.

They made popcorn by the fire. Mandy's grandmother taught her how to knit. Mandy taught her grandmother how to whistle. They had hamburgers and blackberry buckle for supper. In the evening they sat by the fire and whistled and knit.

It was time for Mandy's grandmother to go.

"Will you start casting on for me?" said Mandy. They were sitting in the airport.

"How many stitches?" her grandmother asked.

"I think about a thousand," Mandy said.

"What are we making?" her grandmother asked.

"A blanket for Strawberry," Mandy said.

Mandy's grandmother didn't laugh. She sat in her furry coat and flowered hat, waiting for the airplane to come, smiling and casting on stitches: one, two, three, four.

"I love you, Mandy," her grandmother said.

"I love you, too," said Mandy, because she did.

QUESTIONS

1. Why was Mandy's mother always in a hurry just before Mandy's grandmother visited them?
2. What did Mandy's grandmother bring for Mandy and the baby?
3. Did Mandy like her new dress and hat?
4. Name some of Mandy's favorite things.
5. Tell how Mandy and her grandmother became friends.

The Boy Who Flew Too Close to the Sun

Greek Myth

Many years ago on an island called Crete there lived a wicked king named Minos. Minos had a wife, and his wife was the mother of a strange monster called the *Minotaur*. The Minotaur was half man and half bull.

Minos did not want anybody to know that his wife was the mother of a monster, so he thought of a way to keep it a secret.

He asked a clever man named Daedalus to build a labyrinth. A labyrinth is a place with so many passageways that it is very hard to find one's way out. Daedalus lived in the country of Greece, and he had a little son named Icarus. Together Daedalus and Icarus sailed to Crete to build a labyrinth to keep the Minotaur in. Daedalus built such a good labyrinth that when the Minotaur was placed inside it, he could not find a way out no matter how hard he tried.

King Minos was happy again, and he thanked Daedalus for helping him. But when Daedalus wanted to sail with his son back to Greece, Minos would not let him go. He wanted Daedalus to stay and invent many new things that would help

---

WORDS TO WATCH

Crete	Daedalus	Greece
Minos	labyrinth	Icarus
Minotaur	passageway	prison

him. Minos had Daedalus and Icarus put in prison so that they would have to stay in Crete.

Daedalus and Icarus wanted very much to go home, but they did not know how to escape from prison. Then Daedalus thought of a way to get back home. He said to his little son, "Minos has blocked all my ways of escape by land and by water. But he does not rule the air. We will escape by air. I will make some wings for us, and we will fly back home."

So Daedalus set to work to make wings. He took some feathers and placed them so that the largest feathers were at one end and the smallest feathers at the other. Then he stuck the feathers together with wax so that they looked just like the wings of a large bird. He tied one pair of these wings to his son's arms, and he tied the other pair to his own arms.

Before they tried out their wings, Daedalus said to his son, "Icarus, you must not fly too high nor too low. If you fly too low, you may fall into the sea and drown. If you fly too high, the sun will melt the wax that holds your wings together. The best thing to do is to follow me."

Then they began flapping their wings. At once they rose into the air. Soon they were high above their prison, and they started flying toward home. Icarus was having a good time flying through the air. He forgot all about what his father had told him. Instead of following his father, he flew higher and higher in the sky. He wanted to see how high his wings could carry him. Soon the heat of the sun began to melt the wax. Feathers began to fall off, and his wings began to come apart. Down and down he fell. Icarus kept flapping, but he was flapping only his bare arms. He fell into the sea.

25

Icarus cried out to his father, but the waves closed over him and his cries were heard no more. Daedalus saw some feathers from his little son's wings floating on the water. He flew down and took up the boy's body and flew with it to the shore. There he buried it. Daedalus was heartbroken that he had lost his son and wished that he had never thought of inventing wings.

QUESTIONS

1. Why did Daedalus and his son go to Crete?
2. Why did Minos put Daedalus and Icarus in prison?
3. How did Daedalus make the wings?
4. What did Daedalus tell Icarus not to do?
5. What happened when Icarus did not obey his father?
6. Do you feel more sorry for Daedalus or for Icarus? Why?
7. Write or tell about what you would do if you could fly.
8. Find out more about Crete.

Compound Words

I. Read and Spell

ladybug	outdoors	pancake
sidewalk	airplane	highway
something	penknife	newspaper
skyscraper	grandmother	railroad
tablespoon	strawberry	horseshoe
daylight	afternoon	cannot
bulldog	fireworks	crossroad
turtledove	sunflower	springtime
pigskin	notebook	sheepdog

II. Read and Answer

1. What words are in each of the compound words in Part I?
2. Make three compound words using these words:
   bill   foot   ship   board   ball
3. Think of some more compound words.

III. Write

Write five sentences, each one using a word in Part I.

Love Like Salt

Maria Leach

One day an old king returned from a journey and asked his three daughters if they were glad to see him.

"Your return is like the return of the sun," said the eldest.

"To see you again is like light to my eyes," said the second.

"To have you back is as good as salt," said the youngest.

"WHAT!" said the king to his youngest daughter. "That doesn't sound as though you love me very much."

"I love you as meat loves salt," said the little girl.

This made the king angry, and he scolded her. She was impudent, he said. But she would not change her words.

WORDS TO WATCH		
value	banish	guest
journey	tended	sipped
forgiven	shepherd	knelt
impudent	page	saltcellar

29

So he drove her away. The old king told everybody in his kingdom that he was banishing his youngest daughter because she was impudent and did not love him as much as she should.

The young princess ran out of the house in the night, but she did not know where to go. Suddenly she remembered a little house on the side of a hill where lived a kind old man who tended her father's sheep. He took her in gladly and gave her a bowl of warm milk and bread for her supper and let her lie down to sleep on a soft white sheepskin before the fire. She stayed with the old shepherd a long time after that and helped tend the sheep on the hills.

One day she heard that the king was giving a big feast at the castle. And she decided that she would go and help serve at the table. So she dressed herself in the clothes of a young page and went to the kitchen.

The cook was an old friend of hers who had loved the little princess ever since she was a tiny girl.

"Don't put any salt in anything," she begged the cook. And because the cook thought the old king had it coming to him, he didn't.

When the feast was served, the soup was without salt. The guests sipped at it politely and said nothing. But the king was angry and decided he would have to speak to the cook. When the meat was served, it was tasteless; every dish was without flavor.

So the king did send for the cook. But instead of the cook, a young page came and knelt before the king. "It was my order," said the page. "I thought you did not care for salt."

"And who are you?" said the king.

"I am the child who loves the king like salt," said the girl.

With that the king gave a shout and threw his arms around her. Now he knew the value of salt, and the little princess was forgiven. The servants brought in the saltcellars; the food was salted. The feast went on, and everybody was happy.

QUESTIONS

1. Why did the king think that his youngest daughter did not love him?
2. Where did the princess go after the king turned her out of her home?
3. What did the princess tell the cook to do? Why?
4. What finally made the king know that his daughter really did love him?
5. Do you think that the youngest daughter loved her father more than her sisters did?

The Owl and the Pussy Cat

Edward Lear

The Owl and the Pussycat went to sea
  In a beautiful pea-green boat.
They took some honey, and plenty of money
  Wrapped up in a five-pound note.
The Owl looked up to the stars above,
  And sang to a small guitar,
"Oh lovely Pussy, O Pussy, my love,
  What a beautiful Pussy you are,
    You are,
    You are!
  What a beautiful Pussy you are!"

Pussy said to the Owl, "You elegant fowl,
  How charmingly sweet you sing!
Oh! let us be married; too long we have tarried:
  But what shall we do for a ring?"
They sailed away, for a year and a day,
  To the land where the bong-tree grows,
And there in a wood a Piggy-wig stood,
  With a ring at the end of his nose,
    His nose,
    His nose,
  With a ring at the end of his nose.

"Dear Pig, are you willing to sell for one shilling
  Your ring?" Said the Piggy, "I will."
So they took it away, and were married next day
  By the turkey who lives on the hill.
They dined on mince and slices of quince,
  Which they ate with a runcible spoon;
And hand in hand, on the edge of the sand,
  They danced by the light of the moon,
    The moon,
    The moon,
  They danced by the light of the moon.

David and Goliath

The Bible

Many, many years ago in the land of Israel lived a boy named David. David was very brave and loved God with all his heart.

In those days the people of Israel were at war with the Philistines, who had invaded their country to plunder and steal. The Israelites could not chase the Philistines out of their country, nor could they win a single victory over them. They did not even dare to attack them because they were afraid of Goliath, who was a terrible giant—a man as tall as a tree. His body was covered with armor, and he wore a brass helmet. Every day Goliath walked over to the Israelites and mocked them.

"Come on now," he shouted, "why don't you send over one of your great heroes to fight with me? Are you afraid, you cowards? I am stronger than all of you put together!" And he roared with laughter and cursed the Israelites and also cursed God. Nobody dared to chase him away because everyone trembled with fear just to look at him.

WORDS TO WATCH

Israel	Israelite	mock
Philistine	coward	champion
Goliath	sling	victory
insult	plunder	brass
cursed	fled	swayed

34

David's brothers were soldiers in the Israelite army. One day David went to visit them. Just when he arrived, Goliath was shouting his insults again. David heard him mock the soldiers and curse God, and he became very angry. "Why do you let this giant frighten you?" he asked the soldiers. "Have you forgotten that God is on our side? If no one will fight against Goliath, I will fight him myself."

The soldiers of the Israelites tried to stop him. "Goliath is big and powerful," they said, "and you are only a young boy. You do not even know how to fight."

But these warnings did not stop David. He trusted in God. He remembered when he had guarded his father's sheep. Sometimes a bear or a lion would come out of the woods to steal a lamb. But David had killed each lion and bear, and he knew that God had helped him. He thought to himself, "I will kill Goliath just as I did the bear and the lion, for God will protect me."

When the time came for the fight, Goliath came dressed in his armor and brass helmet, and he carried a spear. At his side he wore a huge sword.

But David did not wear any armor, and instead of a spear and a sword, he had only a sling and five smooth stones.

When Goliath saw David coming without sword or armor, he laughed and shouted, "Whom do we have here? Look at the little boy who cannot even carry a sword! Do you think I am a dog so you can chase me away with your stick? Come on, I'll show you! I'll kill you so that the wild beasts can eat you!" Everybody who heard him speak started trembling with fear, all except David.

David replied, "You come to me with a sword and a spear, but I come to you because you mocked God, and God will give me the victory over you."

Then David put a stone in his sling, took aim, and before Goliath could throw his spear, the stone had hit the giant squarely on the forehead. For a moment Goliath swayed back and forth, and then he fell to the ground.

When the Philistines saw that their champion had been killed by a young boy, they fled in terror. David won a great victory for the people of Israel that day, and years later he became their king.

QUESTIONS

1. Why were the soldiers of Israel afraid to fight Goliath?
2. Why wasn't David afraid to fight Goliath?
3. What did David do when he was guarding his father's sheep to show that he was brave?
4. What did David and Goliath use to fight each other?
5. Why did the Philistines run away?
6. How did the Israelites reward David for his bravery?

Games Children Like

I. Read and Spell

Cards	Chess	Hide-and-Seek
Hopscotch	Tag	Tic-Tac-Toe
Checkers	Gossip	Riddles
Musical Chairs	Hangman	Categories
You Are Getting Hot	Spelling Bee	Tiddlywinks
Dreidel	Jump Rope	Charades
Earth, Fire, Water, and Air	Red Light/ Green Light	Snake / Marbles
Piñata	Stickball	Simon Says
Red Rover	Four-Square	Jacks
Capture the Flag	Captain, May I?	

II. Find Out and Answer

1. How are these games played?
2. Which of these games have you played?
3. Which game do you like to play best?
4. Name some other kinds of games you like.

III. Write

1. Write a story about the game you like most.
2. Explain the rules of one of the games of Part I that you like to play.

Pinocchio

Carlo Collodi

Gepetto lived in a small room with no light except that which came through the doorway. The furniture in his room was very simple: an old chair, a bad bed, and a broken-down table. At the end of the room was a fireplace with a lighted fire, but the fire was painted. Beside the fire was a pot boiling merrily, but the pot was painted on too, and so was the steam that rose from the pot.

Gepetto lived all alone, and sometimes he was very lonely. One day he decided to carve a puppet out of wood so that he

WORDS TO WATCH		
Gepetto	earnestly	clog
fashion	smothered	bawl
puppet	numb	ungrateful
Pinocchio	cobblestone	Carlo Collodi

could have someone to talk to. He got out his tools and set to work to fashion a puppet.

"What name shall I give him?" he said to himself. "I think I will call him Pinocchio. It is a name that will bring him luck. I once knew a whole family by that name. There were Pinocchio the father, Pinocchia the mother, and Pinocchi the children, and all of them did well. The richest of them was a beggar."

After Gepetto found a name for his puppet, he set earnestly to work to make it. First he made the hair, then the forehead, and then the eyes.

The very moment he finished the eyes, he was amazed to see that they moved and that they were staring at him.

"Wicked wooden eyes, why do you stare at me?" he asked.

There was no answer.

Then he began to carve the nose, but no sooner was the nose finished than it began to grow. It grew and grew and grew until it seemed that it would never end. Poor Gepetto kept cutting it off; but the more he cut it off, the more the impudent nose grew.

As soon as the mouth was finished, it began to laugh at Gepetto and make fun of him.

"Stop laughing!" said Gepetto, who was becoming angry. But he might as well have been talking to a wall.

"Stop laughing, I say!" Gepetto roared.

The mouth stopped laughing, but then it stuck out its tongue as far as it would go. Gepetto pretended not to see and went on with his work. After the mouth, he made the chin, then the neck, then the shoulders, the stomach, the arms, and then the hands.

Just as he finished the hands, he felt his wig being snatched from his head. He looked up, and what did he see? He saw his yellow wig in the puppet's hand.

"Pinocchio, give me back my wig!" cried the old man. "Give it back at once."

But instead of giving it back, Pinocchio put it on his own head and almost smothered himself. When Gepetto saw how rude Pinocchio was, he became sadder than he had ever been in his life. He turned to Pinocchio and said to him: "You naughty rascal! You are not even finished yet, and already you have begun to make fun of your poor father. That is bad, my boy, *very bad*." And he wiped away a tear.

Everything was made now, except the legs and feet. The moment that Gepetto finished the feet, he felt a kick on the end of his nose.

"I deserve it!" he said to himself. "I should have thought of it sooner! Now it is too late!"

Gepetto then picked up the puppet and set him on the floor to teach him to walk. Pinocchio's legs were stiff and numb at

first, and he could not move. But Gepetto led him by the hand and showed him how to put one leg in front of the other.

Soon Pinocchio was able to walk by himself and to run around the room. Suddenly he darted through the door, out into the street, and was gone.

Poor Gepetto rushed out after him, but he could not catch him because Pinocchio was running like a scared rabbit. His wooden feet clattered on the cobblestones like the sound of twenty pairs of peasants' clogs.

"Stop him! Stop him!" shouted Gepetto, but the people who saw the puppet running down the street like a race horse were too astonished to do anything. Then they laughed until they could laugh no more.

At last a policeman appeared. He heard the clatter, and thinking that a young horse had got loose, he planted himself in the middle of the street with legs apart. He was determined to stop the runaway and prevent worse things from happening.

When Pinocchio saw the policeman blocking the street ahead of him, he tried to take the policeman by surprise and run underneath his legs. But he failed.

The policeman caught him easily by his long nose and handed him over to Gepetto. Gepetto wanted to punish the puppet by slapping his ears, but to his surprise he discovered that Pinocchio had no ears. In his hurry to make him, Gepetto had forgotten to give him ears.

He then took him by the back of the neck and led him towards his house, all the while saying in a threatening voice, "I will take care of you, young man, when we get home. You can be sure of that."

When Pinocchio heard these words, he threw himself on the ground and would not take another step. Meanwhile a crowd of idle people began to gather around them, talking about Pinocchio. Several of them said, "Poor puppet. No wonder he runs away from home. Who knows how hard that bad old Gepetto beats him!" And others added, "Gepetto seems like a good man, but he doesn't like children. If we leave that puppet in his hands, he may tear him to pieces!"

When the policeman heard all this talk, he turned Pinocchio loose and led Gepetto away to prison. The poor old man could not make the policeman believe what had really happened. All he could do was bawl like a calf.

As he was being led away to prison he cried out, "Ungrateful boy! And to think how hard I worked to make him a good puppet. But it serves me right! I should have thought of it sooner!"

What happens afterward, you will not believe. Do you want to learn how Pinocchio almost gets killed, how he is rescued by a good fairy, how his nose grows longer when he lies, how he turns into a donkey, how he gets swallowed by a terrible whale, and how he turns into a real boy at last? If you do, you can read the whole story in the book called *The Adventures of Pinocchio* by Carlo Collodi.

QUESTIONS

1. What happened when Gepetto made Pinocchio's eyes? What happened when he made his nose? His mouth? His hands? His feet?
2. When Gepetto was leading Pinocchio home, what did the people say?
3. Do you think the policeman made a mistake in setting Pinocchio free and putting Gepetto in jail? Why?

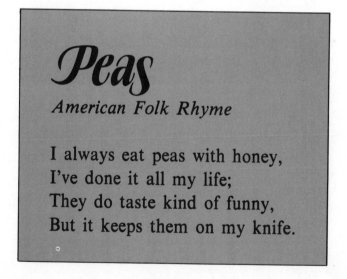

Peas
American Folk Rhyme

I always eat peas with honey,
I've done it all my life;
They do taste kind of funny,
But it keeps them on my knife.

Narcissa

Gwendolyn Brooks

Some of the girls are playing jacks.
Some are playing ball.
But small Narcissa is not playing
Anything at all.

Small Narcissa sits upon
A brick in her back yard
And looks at tiger-lilies,
And shakes her pigtails hard.

First she is an ancient queen
In pomp and purple veil.
Soon she is a singing wind.
And, next, a nightingale.

How fine to be Narcissa,
A-changing like all that!
While sitting still, as still, as still
As anyone ever sat!

45

Animal Names

I. Read and Spell

Animal	Male	Female	Baby
bear	he-bear	she-bear	cub
cow	bull	cow	calf
deer	buck	doe	fawn
elephant	bull	cow	calf
fox	dog	vixen	cub
whale	bull	cow	calf
lion	lion	lioness	cub
goose	gander	goose	gosling

II. Read and Answer

1. What are the babies of these animals called?

   cat   dog   horse   pig   swan   sheep

2. What is the male of these animals called?

   cat   duck   pig   sheep   chicken   horse

3. What is the female of these animals called?

   chicken   tiger   sheep   horse   pig

III. Write

1. Write a story about your favorite animal.
2. Write the funniest story you can remember about your pet or the pet of someone you know.

Snow White and the Seven Dwarfs

Brothers Grimm

Once upon a time a queen sat sewing in front of a window with an ebony frame. It was the middle of the winter, and flakes of snow were falling from the sky like feathers. While the queen was sewing and watching the snow, she pricked her finger with her needle, and three drops of blood fell onto the snow. The crimson color on the white snow looked so beautiful that the queen said to herself, "Oh, if only I had a child with skin as white as snow, with lips as red as blood, and with hair as black as the wood of this ebony frame!"

Some time later she gave birth to a little daughter with skin as white as snow, with lips as red as blood, and with hair as black as ebony. She named the child Snow White. But soon afterward the queen died.

After a year had gone by, the king took another wife. She was beautiful, but proud and haughty and jealous of anyone who seemed to be more beautiful. She had a magic mirror, and whenever she looked at herself in it, she said,

"Mirror, mirror, on the wall,
Who's the fairest one of all?"

WORDS TO WATCH		
envy	startled	falsehood
ebony	endure	rage
crimson	dwarf	mined
mourned	haughty	peasant

Then the mirror replied,

"Lady queen, so grand and tall,
You are the fairest of them all."

And she was satisfied, for she knew the mirror always told the truth.

As time passed, the little child named Snow White grew taller and more beautiful every day, until at last she was more beautiful than the queen herself. So once when the queen asked her mirror,

"Mirror, mirror, on the wall,
Who's the fairest one of all?"

it answered,

"Lady queen, you are tall and grand,
But Snow White is fairest in the land."

Then the queen was startled and turned green with envy. From that hour, she burned with secret envy whenever she saw Snow White.

Finally, she called a huntsman and said, "Take the child into the forest, for I will no longer endure her in my sight. Kill her, and bring back her heart as proof."

The huntsman obeyed and led the child away. But when he had drawn his hunting knife, Snow White began to cry.

The huntsman took pity on her because she looked so lovely and said, "Run away then, poor child!"

As he returned to the castle, the huntsman came upon a bear, which he killed. He then removed its heart and brought it back to the queen, who laughed wickedly when she saw it, believing it to be Snow White's.

The poor child was now all alone in the great dark forest, and she felt frightened as she looked around. She didn't know what to do, so she began to run. She ran over sharp stones and through thorn bushes. Wild animals passed close to her but did her no harm.

She ran as long as her feet could carry her, and when evening came, she saw a little house and went into it to rest.

Everything in the house was very small. There stood a little table, covered with a white tablecloth, on which were seven little plates. There were also seven little spoons, knives, forks, and seven little cups. Up against the walls stood seven little beds with sheets as white as snow.

Snow White was hungry and thirsty, so she ate a little of the vegetables and bread on each plate and drank a little from every cup, because she did not want to eat all of anyone's meal.

Then she grew sleepy, so she lay down in one of the beds, but she could not make herself comfortable, for each bed was either too long or too short. Luckily the seventh bed was just right—so she stayed there, said her prayers, and fell asleep.

When it had grown quite dark, the masters of the house, seven dwarfs who mined for iron among the mountains, came home. They lighted their seven candles, and as soon as there was a light in the kitchen, they saw that someone had been there.

The first said, "Who has been sitting on my chair?"

The second said, "Who has eaten off my plate?"

The third said, "Who has taken part of my bread?"

The fourth said, "Who has touched my vegetables?"

The fifth said, "Who has used my fork?"

The sixth said, "Who has cut with my knife?"

The seventh said, "Who has drunk out of my little cup?"

Then the first dwarf looked around and saw that there was a slight hollow in his bed, so he asked, "Who has been lying in my little bed?"

The others came running, and each called out, "Someone has been lying in my bed too."

But the seventh, when he looked in his bed, saw Snow White there, sound asleep. He called the others, who flocked around with cries of surprise. They fetched their seven candles and cast the light on Snow White. "What a lovely child!" they cried.

The seven dwarfs were so pleased that they would not wake her but let her sleep on in the little bed. The seventh dwarf slept with the others in turn, an hour with each, and so they spent the night.

When morning came, Snow White woke up and was frightened when she saw the seven dwarfs. But they were very friendly to her.

"What is your name?" they asked.

"Snow White," she answered.

"How did you find your way to our house?" the dwarfs asked.

Snow White told them how her stepmother had tried to kill her, how the huntsman had spared her life, and how she had run all day till at last she had found their little house.

Then the dwarfs said, "If you will keep house for us, you may stay here with us."

"Gladly," said Snow White. And so it was agreed.

When the good dwarfs left for the mine in the morning, they warned Snow White. "Beware of your wicked stepmother," they said. "She may soon find out that you are here. Don't let anyone into the house."

The queen, back at the castle, had no doubt that she was again the first and fairest woman in the world. She walked up to her mirror and asked,

"Mirror, mirror, on the wall,
Who's the fairest one of all?"

The mirror replied,

"Lady queen, so grand and tall,
Here, you are fairest of them all;
But over the hills, with the seven dwarfs old,
Lives Snow White, fairer a hundredfold."

The queen trembled with rage, for she knew that the mirror never told a falsehood. So Snow White was still alive!

"Snow White shall die," she cried, "if it costs my own life!"

Then she went to a secret and lonely room where no one ever disturbed her. For hours she stayed in there, making a poisoned apple. Ripe and rosy, it was indeed a beautiful sight to see, but it brought instant death to anyone who ate it.

When the apple was ready, the queen painted her face, disguised herself as a peasant woman, and traveled over the seven hills to where the seven dwarfs lived.

At the sound of the knock, Snow White put her head out of the window and said, "I cannot open the door to anybody. The seven dwarfs have forbidden me to do so."

"Very well," replied the peasant woman. "I only want to get rid of my apples. Here, I will give you one of them!"

"I dare not take it," said Snow White.

"Are you afraid of being poisoned?" said the old woman. "Look here, I will cut the apple in two, and you shall eat the rosy side, and I, the white."

Now the fruit was so cleverly made that only the rosy side

was poisoned. Snow White longed for the pretty apple, and when she saw the peasant woman eating it, she stretched out her hand and took the poisoned half. She had scarcely tasted it when she fell lifeless to the ground.

The queen laughed loudly and watched her for a moment; then she dashed away.

When she got home, she asked the mirror,

> "Mirror, mirror, on the wall,
> Who's the fairest of us all?"

The mirror at last replied,

> "Lady queen, so grand and tall,
> You are the fairest of them all."

When the dwarfs came home in the evening, they found Snow White lying on the ground without any sign of life. They lifted her up and washed her with water and wine, but nothing helped. They tried to waken her, but she did not breathe. She was dead.

They laid Snow White on a bed, sat around her, and wept for three days and three nights. Then they wanted to bury her, but since she looked so beautiful, they decided to place her in a glass case. They carried the case up to the mountain above, and one of them always stayed by it and guarded it. But there was little need to guard it, for even the birds and wild animals came and mourned for Snow White.

For many years Snow White lay unchanged in her glass case, looking as though she were asleep. Her skin was still white as snow, her lips red as blood, and her hair black as ebony.

At last the son of a king chanced to wander into the forest and come to the dwarfs' house for a night's shelter. He saw the case with the beautiful Snow White in it. Then he said to the dwarfs, "Let me have it. I will give you whatever you like for it."

But the dwarfs answered, "We would not part with it for all the gold in the world."

He said again, "Yet give it to me, for I cannot live without seeing Snow White, and though she is dead, I will prize and honor her as my beloved forevermore."

Then the good dwarfs took pity on him and gave him the glass case. The prince lifted it up, but as he did so, a tiny piece of the poisoned apple fell from Snow White's lips. Immediately she opened her eyes and sat up, alive once more. "Where am I?" she asked.

The prince answered joyfully, "With me," and he told her what had happened.

"I love you more dearly than anything else in the world," he said. "Come with me to my father's castle and be my wife." Snow White was well pleased when she heard these words. She went with the prince, and they were married amid much rejoicing.

The wicked stepmother was invited to the feast. She dressed herself in her richest clothes and stood in front of the mirror saying,

"Mirror, mirror, on the wall,
Who's the fairest one of all?"

The mirror answered,

"Lady queen, so grand and tall,
Here, you are fairest of them all;
But the young queen over the mountains old,
Is fairer than you a thousandfold."

The evil-hearted woman could scarcely believe her ears. But curiosity would not allow her to rest. She went to the wedding to see who that young queen could be, who was the most beautiful in all the world. When she came and found that it was Snow White alive again, she tore her hair and stamped away, never to be heard from again, and the handsome prince and Snow White lived happily ever after.

QUESTIONS

1. What did the huntsman do when the queen told him to take Snow White into the forest and kill her?
2. How did the queen learn that Snow White was still alive?
3. How did the queen make the poisoned apple?
4. How did Snow White come to life again after she ate the poisoned apple?
5. What happened to Snow White in the end?
6. What happened to the queen in the end?

Musical Instruments

I. Read and Spell

drum	viola	clarinet
piano	trombone	tuba
flute	accordion	saxophone
trumpet	organ	English horn
cello	piccolo	oboe
harp	guitar	bassoon
kettledrum	French horn	bass viol
bugle	violin	snare drum

II. Read and Answer

1. Which of these instruments are played with a bow?
2. Which of these instruments are played by blowing into them?
3. Which of these instruments are played by striking them?
4. Which of these instruments have keys?
5. Which of these instruments is the smallest?
6. Which is the largest?
7. Name some other musical instruments.
8. If you play an instrument, tell the class which one you play. If not, which one would you like to play?

III. Write

1. Write five sentences, each using a word in Part I.
2. Write a little story telling about the musical instrument you like best.

winnie-the-pooh

A. A. Milne

Edward Bear, known to his friends as Winnie-the-Pooh, or Pooh for short, was walking through the forest one day, humming proudly to himself. He had made up a little hum that very morning, as he was doing his Stoutness Exercises in front of the glass: *Tra-la-la, tra-la-la,* as he stretched up as high as he could go, and then *Tra-la-la, tra-la—oh, help!—la,* as he tried to reach his toes. After breakfast he had said it over and over to himself until he had learned it all by heart, and now he was humming it right through, properly. It went like this:

> *Tra-la-la, tra-la-la,*
> *Tra-la-la, tra-la-la,*
> *Rum-tum-tiddle-um-tum.*

> *Tiddle-iddle, tiddle-iddle,*
> *Tiddle-iddle, tiddle-iddle,*
> *Rum-tum-tum-tiddle-um.*

Well, he was humming this hum to himself and walking along gaily, wondering what everybody else was doing and

---

WORDS TO WATCH

stoutness	mug	convenient
properly	greedy	sigh
scuffling	larder	slenderer
Winnie-the-Pooh	towel-horse	relation

what it felt like, being somebody else, when suddenly he came to a sandy bank, and in the bank was a large hole.

"Aha!" said Pooh. (*Rum-tum-tiddle-um-tum.*) "If I know anything about anything, that hole means Rabbit," he said, "and Rabbit means Company," he said, "and Company means Food and Listening-to-Me-Humming and such like. *Rum-tum-tum-tiddle-um.*"

So he bent down, put his head into the hole, and called out: "Is anybody at home?"

There was a sudden scuffling noise from inside the hole, and then silence.

"What I said was, 'Is anybody at home?' " called out Pooh very loudly.

"No!" said a voice; and then added, "You needn't shout so loud. I heard you quite well the first time."

"Bother!" said Pooh. "Isn't there anybody here at all?"

"Nobody."

Winnie-the-Pooh took his head out of the hole and thought for a little, and he thought to himself, "There must be somebody there, because somebody must have said 'Nobody.' " So he put his head back in the hole and said:

"Hallo, Rabbit, isn't that you?"

"No," said Rabbit, in a different sort of voice this time.

"But isn't that Rabbit's voice?"

"I don't think so," said Rabbit. "It isn't meant to be."

"Oh!" said Pooh.

He took his head out of the hole and had another think, and then he put it back, and said:

"Well, could you very kindly tell me where Rabbit is?"

"He has gone to see his friend Pooh Bear, who is a great friend of his."

"But this is Me!" said Bear, very much surprised.

"What sort of Me?"

"Pooh Bear."

"Are you sure?" said Rabbit, still more surprised.

"Quite, quite sure," said Pooh.

"Oh, well, then, come in."

So Pooh pushed and pushed and pushed his way through the hole, and at last he got in.

"You were quite right," said Rabbit, looking at him all over. "It is you. Glad to see you."

"Who did you think it was?"

"Well, I wasn't sure. You know how it is in the Forest. One can't have *anybody* coming into one's house. One has to be careful. What about a mouthful of something?"

Pooh always liked a little something at eleven o'clock in the morning, and he was very glad to see Rabbit getting out the plates and mugs; and when Rabbit said, "Honey or condensed milk with your bread?" he was so excited that he said, "Both," and then, so as not to seem greedy, he added, "But don't bother about the bread, please." And for a long time after that he said nothing . . . until at last, humming to himself in a rather sticky voice, he got up, shook Rabbit lovingly by the paw, and said that he must be going on.

"Must you?" said Rabbit politely.

"Well," said Pooh, "I could stay a little longer if it—if you—" and he tried very hard to look in the direction of the larder.

"As a matter of fact," said Rabbit, "I was going out myself directly."

"Oh, well, then, I'll be going on. Good-bye."

"Well, good-bye, if you're sure you won't have any more."

"Is there any more?" asked Pooh quickly.

Rabbit took the covers off the dishes and said, "No, there wasn't."

"I thought not," said Pooh, nodding to himself. "Well, good-bye. I must be going on."

So he started to climb out of the hole. He pulled with his front paws, and pushed with his back paws, and in a little while his nose was out in the open again . . . and then his ears . . . and then his front paws . . . and then his shoulders . . . and then—

"Oh, help!" said Pooh. "I'd better go back."

"Oh, bother!" said Pooh. "I shall have to go on."

"I can't do that either!" said Pooh. "Oh, help and bother!"

Now by this time Rabbit wanted to go for a walk too, and finding the front door full, he went out by the back door, and came round to Pooh, and looked at him.

"Hallo, are you stuck?" he asked.

"N-no," said Pooh carelessly. "Just resting and thinking and humming to myself."

"Here, give us a paw."

Pooh Bear stretched out a paw, and Rabbit pulled and pulled and pulled. . . .

"Ow!" cried Pooh. "You're hurting!"

"The fact is," said Rabbit, "you're stuck."

"It all comes," said Pooh crossly, "of not having front doors big enough."

"It all comes," said Rabbit sternly, "of eating too much. I thought at the time," said Rabbit, "only I didn't like to say anything," said Rabbit, "that one of us was eating too much," said Rabbit, "and I knew it wasn't *me*," he said. "Well, well, I shall go and fetch Christopher Robin."

Christopher Robin lived at the other end of the Forest, and when he came back with Rabbit and saw the front half of Pooh, he said, "Silly old Bear," in such a loving voice that everybody felt quite hopeful again.

"I was just beginning to think," said Bear, sniffing slightly, "that Rabbit might never be able to use his front door again. And I should *hate* that," he said.

"So should I," said Rabbit.

"Use his front door again?" said Christopher Robin. "Of course he'll use his front door again."

"Good," said Rabbit.

"If we can't pull you out, Pooh, we might push you back."

Rabbit scratched his whiskers thoughtfully and pointed out that when once Pooh was pushed back, he was back, and of course nobody was more glad to see Pooh than he was, still there it was, some lived in trees and some lived underground, and—

"You mean I'd *never* get out?" said Pooh.

"I mean," said Rabbit, "that having got *so* far, it seems a pity to waste it."

Christopher Robin nodded.

"Then there's only one thing to be done," he said. "We shall have to wait for you to get thin again."

"How long does getting thin take?" asked Pooh anxiously.

"About a week, I should think."

"But I can't stay here for a *week*."

"You can *stay* here all right, silly old Bear. It's getting you out which is so difficult."

"We'll read to you," said Rabbit cheerfully. "And I hope it won't snow," he added. "And I say, old fellow, you're taking up a good deal of room in my house—do you mind if I use your back legs as a towel-horse? Because, I mean, there they are—doing nothing—and it would be very convenient just to hang the towels on them."

"A week!" said Pooh gloomily. "What about meals?"

"I'm afraid no meals," said Christopher Robin, "because of getting thin quicker. But we *will* read to you."

Bear began to sigh and then found he couldn't because he was so tightly stuck, and a tear rolled down his eye, as he said:

"Then would you read a Sustaining Book, such as would help and comfort a Wedged Bear in Great Tightness?"

So for a week Christopher Robin read that sort of book at the north end of Pooh, and Rabbit hung his washing on the south end—and in between Bear felt himself getting slenderer and slenderer. And at the end of the week Christopher Robin said, *"Now!"*

So he took hold of Pooh's front paws, and Rabbit took hold of Christopher Robin, and all Rabbit's friends and relations took hold of Rabbit, and they all pulled together. . . .

And for a long time Pooh only said "Ow!" . . .

And "Oh!" . . .

And then, all of a sudden, he said "Pop!" just as if a cork were coming out of a bottle.

And Christopher Robin and Rabbit and all Rabbit's friends and relations went head-over-heels backwards . . . and on the top of them came Winnie-the-Pooh—free!

So, with a nod of thanks to his friends, he went on with his walk through the forest, humming proudly to himself. But Christopher Robin looked after him lovingly, and said to himself, "Silly old Bear!"

Boa Constrictor
Shel Silverstein

Oh I'm being eaten by a boa constrictor,
A boa constrictor, a boa constrictor,
I'm being eaten by a boa constrictor,
And I don't like it . . . one bit!
Well what do you know . . . it's nibbling my toe,
Oh gee . . . it's up to my knee,
Oh my . . . it's up to my thigh,
Oh fiddle . . . it's up to my middle,
Oh heck . . . it's up to my neck,
Oh dread . . . it's . . . MMFFF.

Some Famous Books

I. Read and Remember

Title	Author
Fables	Aesop
The Adventures of Pinocchio	Carlo Collodi
Peter Pan in Kensington Gardens	J. B. Barrie
Alice's Adventures in Wonderland	Lewis Carroll
Just So Stories	Rudyard Kipling
Fairy Tales	Hans Christian Andersen
Heidi	Johanna Spyri
Robin Hood and Little John	Anonymous
A Child's Garden of Verses	Robert Louis Stevenson
Fairy Tales	The Brothers Grimm
Winnie-the-Pooh	A. A. Milne

II. Find Out and Answer

1. Which of these books have you read?
2. Find out about these books and read one of them.
3. Tell the class about some parts or stories that you remember from one of these books.
4. Find out the titles and authors of other good books.

III. Write

1. Write a report about a book you read and liked.
2. Read one of these books and write a report about it.

Part Two

Famous People

Alexander and His Horse

Greek Legend

A long, long time ago there lived a king named Philip. One day King Philip received a beautiful horse as a present. The king took his new horse out on a wide plain to ride him. He took some of his men with him and also his son Alexander.

But they soon found out that the horse was very wild. It kicked and reared so that no man could mount upon its back. The king was furious that so wild an animal should have been sent to him, and he gave orders for it to be taken back at once.

But Prince Alexander was sorry when he heard this.

WORDS TO WATCH		
Philip	mount	trot
Alexander	gallop	Bucephalus
reared	plain	restless

"It is a pity to lose such a fine horse because no man is brave enough to mount it," said he.

The king thought his son spoke without thinking.

"Your words are bold," he said, "but are you bold enough to mount the horse yourself?"

The young prince went up to the restless animal. He took the bridle and turned its head toward the sun. He did so because he had seen that the horse was afraid of its own black shadow, which kept moving upon the ground before its eyes.

With its face to the sun, the horse could no longer see the shadow, which now fell on the ground behind it. It soon became quiet. Then the prince stroked it and patted it gently, and by and by he sprang quickly upon its back.

The horse at once set off at a gallop over the plain with the boy bravely holding on. The king and his men were in great fear, for they thought the prince would be thrown to the ground and killed. But they need not have been afraid.

Soon the horse grew tired of its gallop and began to trot. Then Alexander turned and gently rode it back. The men shouted, and the king took his son in his arms and shed tears of joy.

The horse was given to the young prince. It loved its master and would kneel down for him to mount, but it would not let any other person get upon its back.

At last, after many years, Alexander's horse was hurt in a fight. But it carried its master to a safe place. Then it lay down and died.

Alexander built a city at that place. He named the city Bucephalus because Bucephalus was the name of his horse.

1. Who was Alexander the Great?
2. Why did Alexander's father not want to keep the horse?
3. Tell how Alexander tamed the horse.
4. How did Alexander show that he was brave?

THE OWL

Anonymous

There was an old owl who lived in an oak;
The more he heard, the less he spoke.
The less he spoke, the more he heard.
Why aren't we like that wise old bird?

Cleopatra

Helen Webber

The kingdom of ancient Egypt lay in northeast Africa and Asia Minor. Its capital city, Alexandria, was a great center of learning. Egypt was called the *gift of the Nile* because each summer that great river flooded its banks and left black soil on the land. The Egyptian farmers planted their crops in this rich soil. Beyond the Nile River valley stretched the desert.

Now the queen of ancient Egypt two thousand years ago was Cleopatra. Cleopatra was the last of the Ptolemies, a family that had ruled Egypt for 300 years. She was intelligent, ambitious, and crafty. She was also so beautiful that she became a legend in her own time.

Cleopatra was just eighteen when she became queen. It was a time when Egypt feared the growing power of Rome. In her public life, Cleopatra wanted to keep power for herself and to keep Egypt strong and free. In her private life, she wanted luxury and love. She tried to make these two parts of her life work together. And, for a while at least, she succeeded. Two great Roman conquerors, Julius Caesar and Mark Antony, made alliances with her and helped to further her plans.

Julius Caesar had conquered much of Europe and then had chased his enemy into Egypt. When he came to the city of Alexandria he met Cleopatra and at once fell in love with her. He took her side in a civil war she was fighting and helped her gain more power in Egypt. They were united, and Cleopatra went back to Rome with Caesar. When Caesar died two years later, she returned to Egypt with their son, Caesarion.

Mark Antony had hoped to inherit all of Caesar's power as Roman emperor, but he had to settle for a part of it. Antony's share of the Roman Empire was in the East, and so he too came to Alexandria. When Cleopatra heard that he was coming, she decided to try to win his heart as she had won Caesar's. She hoped in this way to keep her power in Egypt and perhaps to rule in Rome as well.

She dressed herself as the goddess of love and her maids as nymphs and mermaids. Then she floated down the Nile to meet Antony in a boat so richly ornamented that the people lined the banks of the river for miles just to see her pass.

"The barge she sat in, like a burnished throne,
Burned on the water. . . .
Purple the sails, and so perfumed that
The winds were lovesick with them. The oars were silver,
Which to the tune of flutes kept stroke. . . ."

Antony liked luxury as much as Cleopatra did. And he was as charmed by her beauty and cleverness as Caesar had been. So Antony, too, fell in love with her.

After some years had passed, Antony's followers in Rome grew angry with him for staying in Egypt so long and for marrying Cleopatra. Another powerful Roman leader, Octavian, made war on Antony and Cleopatra. Octavian's fleet defeated the fleets of Antony and Cleopatra at the great naval battle of Actium. Then the couple fled to Alexandria, followed by Octavian. And here their ambitions and their love came to a bitter end.

Antony was led to believe that Cleopatra had taken her own life, so he threw himself on his sword. When he heard that she was really alive, he had himself carried into her presence. Then he spoke to her: "I am dying, Egypt, dying. . . ." She took him in her arms and there he died. Then Cleopatra took a poisonous snake on her arm and let it bite her. She was buried beside Antony. Her death marked the start of Roman rule in Egypt.

Twenty centuries have passed since the time of Cleopatra, but poets and painters through the ages have been fascinated by her story and have told or pictured it in a great many ways. For as the greatest of our poets, Shakespeare, said of Cleopatra: "Age cannot wither her, nor custom stale her infinite variety."

QUESTIONS

1. Why was Egypt called the "gift of the Nile"?
2. What did Cleopatra want in her public life? In her private life?
3. How did Cleopatra prepare to meet Antony?
4. How did Cleopatra and Antony die?
5. On a map, find Rome, Egypt, the Nile River, and Alexandria.
6. Find out more about the Roman Empire, Julius Caesar, Mark Antony, and Octavian.

William Tell

Swiss Legend

Switzerland is a beautiful little country in Europe. A long time ago it was conquered by the Austrians, and a wicked, cruel Austrian named Gessler ruled over the Swiss people. Although Gessler had many soldiers, he could not make the proud Swiss bow down when he passed by.

Boiling with rage, he thought of a way to make them feel his power. In the market place of the village of Altdorf, he set up a high pole and placed his Austrian hat on top of it. He ordered every Swiss man, woman, and child to bow to the hat whenever they passed by it.

One day William Tell came down from his home in the mountains to visit friends in Altdorf. He was tall and strong, known as the finest archer in the country, who could shoot bears and wolves with his crossbow. With him was his only son, a boy ten years old.

They crossed the market place and passed by the pole, but they did not bow. At once several soldiers surrounded Tell and took him before Gessler.

"Why did you not bow to the hat?" asked Gessler.

WORDS TO WATCH		
market place	Europe	Altdorf
Austria	measured	tyrant
Switzerland	power	dungeon
crossbow	pale	rudder
paces	country	spared

"I am a Swiss," replied Tell. "I do not have to bow to an Austrian hat."

"Bow or die," shouted Gessler.

"I would sooner die than bow to it," replied Tell proudly.

Then Gessler, who could hardly control his mounting anger, thought of something else.

"They tell me you shoot very well," he said with a wicked smile. "I will not punish you. Instead, we will see if you are as good as people say you are. Let your son stand a hundred paces from you. Put an apple on his head, and shoot an arrow through the apple. If you fail, you shall be put to death; if you succeed, your life will be spared."

"I'd rather die than aim an arrow at my own son," cried Tell. "You cannot ask a father to do such a horrible thing."

"Do as I order," shouted Gessler furiously, "or I'll put both you and your son to death!"

All the people who heard these words turned pale with fear, and other fathers held their sons close to them. But the little boy whispered to his father, "I am not afraid, Father. I will hold very still, and I will not even breathe or blink an eye."

Gessler's soldiers measured off the hundred paces, led the boy to the marked spot, and placed an apple on his head.

William Tell slowly took out two arrows, slipped one under his belt, and fitted the other to his crossbow. His son held his head high and stood motionless while he watched his father bend the crossbow and take aim. The crowd did not dare to breathe. Zing! The arrow sped from the crossbow, straight to the apple, and split it in two pieces. Not a hair of the boy's head was touched. The crowd cheered; everyone was overjoyed.

"A master shot," cried Gessler, "but tell me, did you not put a second arrow under your belt?"

"The second arrow was for you, if my son had been hurt," replied Tell.

"I gave my word to spare your life," shouted the Austrian furiously, "but I will teach you a lesson. Bind him," he ordered, "and take him across the lake to my castle. Throw him in the dungeon, where he will see neither sun nor moon as long as he lives. Then I shall be safe from his arrows!"

The soldiers bound William Tell with ropes and threw him into the bottom of a boat. When they were in the middle of the lake, a terrible storm arose, and the soldiers set Tell free so that he could help them with the boat. He took the rudder and steered the boat toward the rocks. As soon as they were close enough, he suddenly sprang ashore, kicking the boat back into the wild waves of the lake.

Tell escaped into the mountains, which no one else knew as well as he. He hid near the path which Gessler had to take to his castle, and he waited. His second arrow was ready, fitted to the crossbow. When Gessler passed by late that afternoon, the arrow did not miss, and the wicked tyrant fell dead.

Two Cats

Anonymous

There once were two cats of Kilkenny,
Each thought there was one cat too many;
So they fought and they fit,
And they scratched and they bit,
Till, excepting their nails
And the tips of their tails,
Instead of two cats, there weren't any.

Boadicea

Judith Barnard

More than 1,900 years ago, in 62 A.D., a huge army fought its way across Britain. The army was from Rome. It was part of an even greater army that was conquering countries all over Europe and even in Africa and Asia.

At that time, Britain had small, crowded towns instead of cities. Groups of people lived in tribes, each with its own name, each with its cluster of huts separated from other tribes by rough ground or marshes. Until the Roman soldiers came, there were few roads. The Romans built roads for their armies to move quickly as they defeated one tribe after another. When Roman soldiers marched along the roads, the earth shook, and the tramp-tramp-tramp of heavy feet could be heard for miles.

Roman troops became known for their cruelty to the people they had conquered. They took money and animals and food, often leaving nothing for the families they robbed. When crops were ready for harvest, the soldiers moved in and took what they wished from the fields; they left behind stripped plants or the poor crops they didn't want.

The soldiers made free with the people's homes, walking into huts where people ate or slept, taking women and children. There were no laws to protect the people; the only law was Roman force of arms. The people were always afraid, always angry—and always helpless.

But the people of the Iceni tribe thought they might not be

so helpless after all. They were one of the largest tribes; and they were a proud and hard-working people. Often they refused when Roman soldiers demanded food or higher taxes. For a while, their refusals brought only harsher treatment from the Romans. So the Iceni went to their queen to tell her they wanted to rebel.

The queen was Boadicea. The king had died the year before. After his death, the Romans became bolder in their demands, as if they felt a widowed queen could do nothing to stop them.

But Boadicea knew that a king or queen sometimes *follows* the people, as well as leading them. When her people talked of rebellion she could not ask them to be patient. And besides, she too was angry. She stood and held out her hands. "We will make our own weapons," she said. "Others we will steal from the Romans while they sleep. And we will drive out every Roman soldier. The land will be ours again!"

Thousands of Iceni men and women armed themselves with battering rams, catapults, stones, javelins, swords, and daggers. People from other tribes joined them. Howling great war cries that echoed in the cool dawn shadows, they attacked the Roman camp near London.

By nightfall, as the sun disappeared, twisted bodies covered the ground. Bushes were red with the blood of Roman and Iceni soldiers. The air was heavy and hushed; no birds sang, no dogs barked. Boadicea led her survivors back to camp. "We won this battle," she thought, "but we will lose in the end. Too many of our fighters were killed. The Romans have smaller armies but they have better weapons and they have training; we have none. But what else can we do?"

There was nothing else they could do. They fought on, and at first they won several important battles. The Iceni drove the Romans out of London, out of Colchester, out of Verulamium (later called St. Albans). A feeling of freedom and victory was everywhere. People slept at night without trembling at every sound, without wondering when Romans would steal women or children, or take all the food and animals for themselves.

But as Boadicea had foreseen, the victories did not last. Suetonius Paulinus, a Roman general, alarmed by the Iceni march that was driving Roman soldiers into retreat, led his army against Boadicea's army. The Romans crushed the Iceni; they crushed the tribal army beneath their feet. It seemed they would crush the last living things in Britain.

Finally the Roman soldiers reached Boadicea's camp and killed the Iceni guarding her. The Romans captured the queen and made plans to take her to Rome.

But Boadicea had no intention of going to Rome. Her armies were defeated, her land lay in ruins. Roman troops occupied every town. There was no escape, there would be no freedom, no more victories. But she belonged in Britain, not in Rome.

That night, alone in her prison hut, Boadicea took from a hiding place a poison she had been saving for the defeat she had foreseen. She held it up and then, without taking a moment to think, quickly swallowed it all.

In the morning, when the soldiers came to take her to the ship, she lay on the floor, very cold, very still. There was nothing the soldiers could do. Boadicea was dead; she would never be a slave of Rome.

QUESTIONS

1. Was Boadicea wise to keep fighting after she knew the Iceni could not win?
2. Why was the Roman army better than the Iceni army?
3. Find out more about the Romans in Britain. Who was Julius Caesar? What is Hadrian's Wall?

Happy Thought

Robert Louis Stevenson

The world is so full of a number of things,
I'm sure we should all be as happy as kings.

Occupations

I. Read and Spell

teacher	lawyer	plumber
doctor	police officer	physicist
nurse	chemist	carpenter
engineer	scientist	fire fighter
librarian	politician	banker
office worker	mechanic	photographer
professor	journalist	salesclerk
executive	veterinarian	farmer
astronaut	factory worker	interpreter
writer	merchant	soldier
architect	artist	pilot
sailor	musician	actor

II. Read and Answer

1. Tell what people do in each of these occupations.
2. What kind of education do you need for each of these occupations?
3. Name some other occupations.
4. What do you think you might like to be?
5. How would you prepare yourself for your work?
6. Can a woman be a police officer, a physicist, or a carpenter?

III. Write

1. Write five sentences, each using a word in Part I.
2. Write a story about what you want to be when you are grown up.

Mary Queen of Scots

Mary Stuart was born in Scotland over 400 years ago, in the days when Scotland and England were still separate kingdoms. She was crowned Queen of Scotland upon the death of her father, the king, when she was only one week old.

At the age of five, the child-queen was sent to the court of France to be educated. There she met the crown prince of France, who was to be her future husband. The two children grew up together as friends. They were married when Mary had become a tall and lovely girl of 15. The French people loved her for her sweetness and beauty. Many French poets wrote verses in praise of her.

By the time Mary was 16 her young husband had become king, and she had become the queen of France as well as of Scotland. But before a year had passed she was a widow. Mary had led a happy and protected young life. What lay ahead of her now was sorrow and tragedy.

She decided to return to the Scotland she had almost forgotten. There she missed the mild weather of France. She missed the music and dancing and other pleasant customs of the French court. Most painful of all, she found that her Catholic faith was out of favor in Scotland, which was becoming Protestant during her years in France.

Queen Mary tried to allow freedom of religion to all her people. But the people had not yet learned to respect each other's beliefs. The leader of the Protestants frowned on Mary, her church, and her customs. He complained that wicked Mary had "danced past midnight out of glee." The

Catholics, for their part, wanted Mary to restore their power and drive the Protestants out. Nothing she did really satisfied either side.

The troubles in Scotland turned into violent rebellion. Mary was captured by some of the Protestant nobles. She was imprisoned in a dark, grim castle on an island in the middle of a lake.

In disguise, Mary escaped from the island. She quickly raised a small army. But her army was defeated, and she had to flee. She might have fled to France, where she had friends and property. Instead, she sailed to England in a fishing boat and asked protection from her cousin, Queen Elizabeth I. This was Mary's worst mistake. Once in England she was drawn into Queen Elizabeth's spider web.

Elizabeth feared that Mary was plotting to make herself queen of England. So she had Mary put in prison. Mary suffered 19 long years in prison, broken in health. It was there that her religion became a great comfort to her. She gained peace of spirit at the cost of much pain.

At last, Elizabeth charged that Mary had plotted against her life. Mary was tried, found guilty, and beheaded. The courage and dignity with which she faced death has since become a legend.

The motto of Mary Queen of Scots was: "In my end is my beginning." Although Mary herself died an outcast, Scotland and England were united under the rule of her son, King James I. Every ruler of Britain since that time has been descended from her. So the end of Mary Stuart was the beginning of a long line of Stuart kings and queens.

A Good Thanksgiving

Marian Douglas

Said old Gentleman Ray, "On Thanksgiving day,
If you want a good time, then give something away."

So he sent a fat turkey to Shoemaker Price,
And the shoemaker said, "What a big bird! How nice.

"With such a good dinner before me, I ought
To give Widow Lee the small chicken I bought."

89

"This fine chicken, oh, see!" said the pleased Widow Lee,
"And the kindness that sent it, how precious to me.

"I would like to make someone as happy as I—
I'll give Washerwoman Biddy my big pumpkin pie."

"And oh sure!" Biddy said, " 'tis the queen of all pies!
And to look at its yellow face gladdens my eyes.

"Now it's my turn, I think; and a sweet ginger cake
For the motherless Finigan children I'll bake."

Said the Finigan children—Rose, Denny, and Hugh—
"It smells sweet of spice, and we'll carry a slice
To poor little lame Jake, who has nothing that's nice."

"Oh I thank you, and thank you," said the little lame Jake.
"What a beautiful, beautiful, beautiful cake!

"And such a big slice! I will save all the crumbs,
And give them to each little sparrow that comes."

And the sparrows they twittered, as if they would say,
Like old Gentleman Ray, "On Thanksgiving day,
If you want a good time, then give something away."

Holidays

I. Read and Remember

New Year's Day

Lincoln's Birthday

Valentine's Day

Passover

Easter Sunday

Memorial Day

Flag Day

Washington's Birthday

Martin Luther King's Birthday

Hanukkah

Independence Day

Labor Day

Rosh Hashanah

Christmas Day

Halloween

Columbus Day

Thanksgiving Day

Chinese New Year

St. Patrick's Day

II. Read and Answer

1. Why are these holidays celebrated?
2. When are these holidays celebrated?
3. How are these holidays celebrated?

III. Read and Write

Write a story about your favorite holiday.

Father Hidalgo

Helen Webber

In Mexico, our neighboring country to the south, September 16 is Independence Day. Each year on the eve of that day, the people of Mexico City gather in front of the president's palace. The president rings the liberty bell and gives the famous call, "Long live independence! Long live Mexico!" The people answer, shouting "*Viva* Mexico! Long live Mexico!" Then, perhaps, parents will tell their children why the liberty bell was brought to the palace from the church in Dolores, and how the priest of that church, Father Hidalgo, became the father of his country.

Father Hidalgo was the son of a Spanish family, and the Spanish had ruled Mexico for three hundred years. But he had been born in Mexico, and his heart was with the Mexican people. Although he was an educated man who had taught in a college, he chose to be a priest in the little village of Dolores. There the people were poor and hungry. Father Hidalgo was a strong and lively man, and one who loved a joke. But he was no longer young when he began the great work of his life.

He had many good ideas for helping his flock to learn trades that he hoped would lift them out of their poverty. He taught them how to grow grapes for making wine and how to grow mulberry trees and stock them with silkworms for making silk. But when the Spanish rulers heard of the priest's work, they sent men to destroy the crops. Mexicans were not

to be allowed to make wine and silk. Instead, they had to buy these things from Spain, at high prices that none but the rich could pay.

Then Father Hidalgo started a blacksmith's shop. He also taught brickmaking and pottery and other crafts to the people of Dolores. But progress was slow, and they still did not have enough to eat. He began to believe that Mexico must free herself from Spain. Other men and women shared his belief. Talk of freedom was everywhere. Together with his friends, the priest started to plan an uprising, but the Spanish found out about these plans. It was dangerous now to delay.

Father Hidalgo decided to act at once. His first thought was to ask the Virgin of Guadalupe, a saint much loved by poor Mexicans, to bless his attempt to free Mexico. Ringing his church bell—the same bell that became Mexico's liberty bell—he called the people from their homes to meet at the church. There he prayed to the Virgin and then spoke to the people he loved. He ended his speech with the call to independence that would be shouted throughout Mexico every September for years to come. "*Viva* Mexico!"

Then the priest, followed by a dozen men of Dolores, set out to raise an army. They walked from town to town, and soon the ragged band numbered eighty thousand men. They were armed mostly with sticks, stones, knives, and axes. Under the banner of the Virgin of Guadalupe, they fought the Spanish army. It is said that some of the Mexicans knew so little about fighting that they tried to stop the Spanish cannons by holding straw hats over the mouths of the cannons. But their desire for freedom made them fight on.

At first the Mexicans won battle after battle. Later, however, they could not stand up against the well-trained and well-armed Spanish soldiers. After a year of fighting, Father Hidalgo was captured and put to death. But the fight for freedom did not die with him. After ten more years, the Mexicans finally won their independence.

Although he did not live to see Mexico free from Spanish rule, perhaps Father Hidalgo guessed that Mexicans would one day govern themselves and would remember him as the father of their independence. Not only have the Mexicans remembered Father Hidalgo, they have also brought his church bell from Dolores to their capital city and made it their liberty bell.

QUESTIONS

1. Describe the Independence Day celebrations in Mexico.
2. How was Father Hidalgo's uprising against the Spanish like the American Revolution?
3. Find out something about the American liberty bell, which is now in Philadelphia.

The Lady with the Lamp

Margaret Leighton

Already as a little girl, Florence Nightingale took care of her sick dolls and pets. When she was a bit older, she visited and nursed the sick and poor people in her village. She loved her parents and her sister dearly, but she did not care about beautiful clothes, elegant parties, travel, and all the other things that her family enjoyed. More than anything she wanted to become a nurse! At that time, though, there were no nurses as we now know them. Hospitals in England and all over the world were the most horrible places one can imagine. Sick people would not think of going there if they could find anyone to nurse them at home. Hospitals were dirty and overrun by lice and fleas. The women who worked in them were uneducated and looked down upon. That's why Florence's parents did not allow her to work in a hospital. But Florence was strong-willed and determined. She secretly read and studied all she could find about hospitals and nursing. After many unhappy years, Florence got her way. She managed one hospital in London so successfully that she was called to serve when war broke out between England and Russia. She took 38 nurses to the Crimea to organize hospitals and nursing for the wounded soldiers. The following story begins the day after their arrival in the Crimea.

Florence Nightingale and her nurses slept very little that night. They were all cold and hungry. Fleas bit them, the wooden benches were hard, and rats ran about the room all night.

Florence rose in the early dawn and looked out at the bright sky.

Already she had made her plans. "We will set up the portable stoves which we brought from Marseilles in here," she told her nurses. "We will make hot, nourishing drinks and have them ready for the wounded when they are brought here from the ships."

The stretchers, loaded with sick and wounded soldiers, soon began to pour into the hospital. Miss Nightingale and her nurses were working in the wards, cleaning, dressing wounds, and caring for the sick.

The commander of the army sent word that five hundred more wounded men were being sent down from the fighting front to the Scutari hospitals.

"But there's no space left even on the floor!" exclaimed the officer in charge of the hospitals, when he heard this news.

"A whole wing of the Barrack Hospital is not in use," Florence said quietly. "I'm told it was destroyed by fire. Why not repair it?"

The officer shook his head. "That fire happened before we took this place over," he exclaimed. "I have no right to have repairs made there. I'd have to get permission from the War Office in London."

"I shall have it done myself, then," said Florence Nightingale. She hired workmen, bought lumber and supplies, and drew up plans. By the time the ships arrived bringing the wounded, the new wing was ready for them.

But still the disasters grew. The British Army had failed to supply its troops with warm clothing or proper food. Winter came. The men suffered cruelly in the icy trenches from

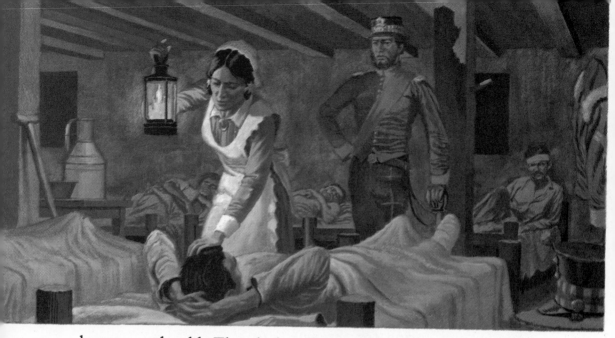

hunger and cold. The cholera increased. More than half the Army lay wounded and sick. The Nightingale nurses worked from before dawn to after dark with quiet heroism.

But night did not bring an end to Florence Nightingale's labors.

One night a young transport sailor named William lay restless and wakeful in his cot. It was almost midnight. The great echoing wards of the Barrack Hospital were dark. The only sound was the slow step of the sentry pacing the stone floor.

William's throat burned with thirst. The pain of his shattered leg seemed more than he could bear. Worst of all was the fear growing in his heart.

"Tomorrow we'll operate," the surgeon had said.

"What does that mean?" William wondered. "Will they cut my leg off? I think I'd rather die, here and now!"

Suddenly he noticed shadows sliding along the ceiling. A light was moving, far down the ward. A whispered murmur passed from man to man. "It's *her!* It's Nurse Nightingale," they said.

She came as quietly as a shadow. When she reached William's cot she set the lantern down and bent over him. Her cool hand touched his forehead. "You're hot and thirsty, William. Here's a drink for you."

Her arm steadied him while he gulped the water. "There, is that better?" she asked. In the lantern light her face was pale, but as kind and gentle as his own mother's.

"Nurse Nightingale," William said hoarsely, "are they going to cut off my leg tomorrow?"

Florence Nightingale's face was grave. "I don't know, William," she said. "But I promise you that I shall be there with you all the time. If they can save your leg, they will, you may be sure of that. And will you promise me something?"

"What do you mean, ma'am?" he asked doubtfully.

"Promise me that you will bear whatever they decide like the brave British sailor that you are," she asked.

He could not refuse *her*. "Yes, I'll promise," he said.

She smiled. "Now try to sleep." She touched his eyelids and he closed them. But when she moved on, he raised his head and watched the light of her lantern flickering down the long room. She spoke to a soldier here, and smiled at another there. William saw a brawny fellow turn his head and kiss her shadow as it lay for a moment on his pillow.

"She seems to know, somehow, whenever a fellow is a bit low, and she comes to cheer him up," the man next to William said. "She's an angel, and no mistake."

William turned over on his side. He could still feel the touch of her fingers on his eyelids. And what Florence Nightingale did for him that night she did for hundreds, yes, thousands of other men during that terrible and tragic winter.

The Coming of Morning

Emily Dickinson

Will there really be a morning?
  Is there such a thing as day?
Could I see it from the mountains
  If I were as tall as they?

Has it feet like water lilies?
  Has it feathers like a bird?
Is it brought from famous countries
  Of which I have never heard?

Oh, some scholar! Oh, some sailor!
  Oh, some wise man from the skies!
Please do tell a little pilgrim
  Where the place called morning lies!

Martin Luther King

Every American child learns in school that black people were first brought to this country as slaves. It took a bloody civil war to set them free. But perhaps not everyone knows that a hundred years after the Civil War, black Americans still did not have the right to live and work and play and go to school where they liked. The story of how they worked to gain these rights—which we call *civil rights*—is partly the story of a young minister named Martin Luther King. He became a hero to black people, as well as to a great many other people who care about freedom and peace. The events that were to make Martin Luther King a fighter for civil rights began in Montgomery, Alabama, on a winter day in 1955.

That day a black woman named Rosa Parks was riding a bus home. She was tired after a long day's work. In 1955, the law in Montgomery was that black people had to sit in the back of the bus. They also had to give up their seats if white passengers were standing. When the bus that Rosa Parks was riding became crowded, the driver ordered her to give her seat to a white man. With quiet courage, she refused. Then the police came and arrested her.

WORDS TO WATCH		
civil	nonviolence	content
boycott	injustice	refuse
weary	racial	Montgomery

Black people were very angry to hear how Mrs. Parks had been treated. They knew that the law was wrong. They were tired of being treated unjustly because of their race. They decided to *boycott* the buses—to refuse to ride in them at all. If all the black people of Montgomery refused to ride in the buses, the bus company would make a lot less money.

Martin Luther King led this boycott, talking to his followers to give them strength and hope whenever they grew weary. For a whole year, thousands of blacks refused to ride the buses. Instead, they went to their jobs any way they could—some even riding mules, and many walking for miles. News of the Montgomery bus boycott spread all over America. Many people everywhere agreed with the blacks of Montgomery and did what they could to help change the laws. And, of course, the bus company made less money. At last the fighters for civil rights won, and the unjust bus laws were changed. Martin Luther King was proud that his people had won their victory without using any violence.

His belief in *nonviolence*—in the power of using peaceful means to attack injustice—was the idea that ruled his life. No matter how often he was the target of hate and violence, he never allowed himself or his followers to use violence in return. The fighters for civil rights went from victory to victory over racial injustice, both in the South and in the North. Martin Luther King went with them, walking at the front of his peaceful army wherever there was danger to face and a wrong to make right. He was even willing to go to jail many times for breaking those laws that he knew to be unjust. By the time his short life was over, there were people all over the country—indeed, all over the world—who believed in his ideas and wanted to carry on his work.

In 1963, the fighters for civil rights had a March on Washington to mark the hundredth anniversary of the freeing of the slaves. They wanted to remind the government that much work was still to be done. On that summer day, a quarter of a million people, black and white, stood before the Lincoln Memorial and heard Martin Luther King say:

I have a dream today. I have a dream that my four little children will one day live in a nation where they will not be judged by the color of their skin but by the content of their character. . . . When we let freedom ring, when we let it ring from every village and every town, from every state and every city, we will be able to speed up the day when all of God's children, black men and white men, . . . will be able to join hands and sing in the words of that old Negro song, "Free at last! Free at last! Thank God Almighty, we are free at last!"

Some Famous People of the World

I. Read and Spell

Plato	Dante	Mozart
Aristotle	Shakespeare	St. Frances Cabrini
Cleopatra	Leonardo da Vinci	Goethe
Julius Caesar	Bach	Darwin
Archimedes	Newton	Jane Austen
Napoleon	Marie Curie	Chief Joseph
Confucius	José Martí	Helen Keller
Chopin	Pablo Casals	Gregor Mendel
Mahatma Gandhi	Golda Meir	Max Planck
Geronimo	Lao-tze	Nefertiti
Joan of Arc	Lady Murasaki	Garibaldi
Toussaint L'Ouverture		Yuri Gagarin
Joseph Jenkins Roberts		Michelangelo

II. Find Out and Answer

1. Find out why ten of these people are famous.
2. Think of some other famous people.
3. Find out the names of some people who are famous as:
   - a. poets
   - b. scientists
   - c. world leaders
   - d. painters
   - e. composers
4. What makes people famous?
5. Can a person be great without being famous?

III. Write

1. Write a story about a famous person you like.
2. Write a story about what you would most like to be famous for.

Part Three

Science and
Nature

A B C D E F G
H I J K L M
N O P Q R S T
U V W X Y Z

THE WONDERFUL ALPHABET

Did you know that one of the most wonderful inventions in the world is our alphabet? Who would ever imagine that these twenty-six little letters could be so important?

Do you think you could write a letter to a friend inviting him to visit you if you could not use the alphabet? Perhaps you could do it with pictures, but it wouldn't be very easy. Your friend might even misunderstand the letter and think that you were coming to visit him!

Yet thousands of years ago, people did write with pictures because no alphabet had been invented. Instead of writing "sun," they would draw a circle. A few straight lines might

---

WORDS TO WATCH

misunderstand	Phoenician	German
Chinese	Spanish	Roman
alpha	French	Russia
beta		

mean "trees" or "forest." A few wavy lines might mean "water," or "lake," or "ocean." This is writing the hard way, and many ideas were not easy to write with pictures. For example, it would be hard to say with pictures, "the boys looked like good boys but were really bad boys."

The ancient Egyptians could do many amazing things, but they also used picture writing because they did not have an alphabet. So did many Indian tribes in America.

Some of the peoples of the world wrote with signs instead of pictures. Sometimes the signs looked a little bit like the thing they stood for. In Chinese, for example, the sign for

man is 人 , which looks a little bit like a man walking;

and 木 , which means "tree" or "wood" in Chinese,

looks a little like a tree with some branches. But in Chinese and some other languages like Chinese, there are thousands and thousands of these signs, all different. Most of them don't look at all like the things they stand for.

Did you ever stop to think how our alphabet was invented? The word "alphabet" comes from the words "alpha" and "beta," which are the Greek letters for A and B. But the Greeks did not invent our alphabet. The Phoenicians invented it. The Phoenicians lived a long time ago and were great sailors and traders. They traded with many countries across the seas, and in buying and selling, they needed a fast way of writing things down. So they invented signs that stood for the sounds of their language. In this way our alphabet began. The Greeks learned the alphabet from the Phoenicians, and the people of western Europe learned it from the Greeks.

Today most languages have alphabets. Many alphabets are quite different from ours, but they are just as useful. In recent years, the Chinese have made their own alphabet. People in Russia, Iran, India, and elsewhere each have their own alphabets. The alphabet of English and Spanish and French and German and many other languages is called the Roman alphabet because it hasn't changed much since the days of ancient Rome.

In German the word "tree" is written "Baum"; in French it is written "arbre"; and in Spanish it is "árbol," but the letters are written the same way that they are in English.

But no matter what the language may be, if it has an alphabet, it is easier to write the word for tree than to draw a picture.

QUESTIONS

1. How did people write before an alphabet was invented?
2. Where does the word "alphabet" come from?
3. How was our alphabet invented?
4. Name some languages that have the same letters as English.
5. Name some languages that have letters different from English.
6. Would you rather write with pictures or with the alphabet? Why?
7. Write a sentence using only pictures, and see if the rest of the class can read what you wrote.

The Invention of Printing

Hundreds of years ago there were no printed books like the one you are reading now. In olden times books were written in "manuscript," which means that they were written by hand.

The books were copied carefully and were very beautiful. It often took a person two to three years to finish one hand-written book. Therefore books were expensive, and only a few people could buy them and learn about the world the way you can today.

Though the people of Europe didn't know it, printing had been invented by the Chinese. The Chinese would carve the symbol for a word on a block of wood. This symbol had to be carved backwards. Then the wood was dipped in ink or paint, placed on a piece of paper, and pressed down. When the block was raised, the word would be on the paper—right side around.

WORDS TO WATCH

Johann Gutenberg	expensive	printing press
manuscript	movable type	improvement

Years later in Europe, printers would carve an entire page on wood. Every letter, word, and sentence had to be backwards! Then the whole page was covered with ink. Large machines worked by hand were built to hold these wooden pages and to press them to paper. These machines are called printing presses.

Different printers began making small, separate blocks for each letter of the alphabet. The letters were then put together to spell words. If enough letters were made for the words on a page, the whole page could then be inked and printed. By using more ink, many copies of a page could be printed. Then each letter was removed and used over again to form new words for another page of a book. Books were now much easier and cheaper to make.

In time, the letter blocks were made of metal. We call these blocks "type." What these printers were using was "movable type"—just as the Chinese had been doing for years.

A German named Johann Gutenberg was one of the first printers in Europe to use movable type and the printing press. Some of the oldest printed material in Europe was made by

him. He is often thought of as the inventor of the printing press, mainly because we don't know the names of many other early European printers.

The first book that we believe Gutenberg and his helpers printed was the Bible. It is a very beautiful example of the printer's art. Today a copy of the Gutenberg Bible is very valuable.

Soon books were printed all over Europe. For the first time, many people could read about faraway places, and the poets and thinkers of long ago were brought back to life.

The Gutenberg Bible was printed a little before Columbus discovered America. Since then, many improvements have been made on printing presses. Today printing presses can print thousands of books in an hour. Books, magazines, and newspapers are all printed on printing presses.

For very little money, you can buy enough newspapers and magazines and books to keep you busy reading for a whole week. And for nothing at all, at your public library you can read books on every subject you can think of.

Did you ever think that one invention could be so important?

QUESTIONS

1. How were books made before the printing press was invented?
2. What is movable type?
3. Why was the invention of the printing press important?
4. How could the printing press bring the poets and thinkers of long ago back to life?
5. Did you ever visit a library to see all the interesting books?
6. Why is the letter on a piece of type backwards?

The International System of Units (Metric System)

I. Read and Spell

Length	*Weight (Mass)*	*Volume*
millimeter	milligram	milliliter
centimeter	centigram	centiliter
decimeter	decigram	deciliter
meter	gram	liter
dekameter	dekagram	dekaliter
hectometer	hectogram	hectoliter
kilometer	kilogram	kiloliter

II. Find Out and Answer

1. What does the prefix *milli-* mean? What does the prefix *kilo-* mean? What do they both mean in the Metric System?
2. What do the prefixes *centi-, deci-, deka-,* and *hecto-* mean? What meaning do they have in the Metric System?
3. How many cents are there in a dollar?
4. How many centigrams are there in a gram? Centimeters in a meter? Centiliters in a liter?
5. How many meters are there in a kilometer? How many grams are there in a kilogram?
6. What does the word *decathlon* mean? What does the word *millipede* mean?
7. Why is the Metric System of Units easy to use?

Copernicus and Galileo

On the morning of a clear day, you can see the sun rising in the east; and in the evening, you can see it going down in the west. This makes you think that the sun is going around the earth. And this is why, long ago, most people used to think that the sun went around the earth. They thought that the stars and the planets moved around the earth in big circles. They thought that our earth was the center of these circles.

WORDS TO WATCH		
planet	movement	telescope
Copernicus	Galileo	

But a man named Copernicus did not believe that the sun went around the earth. He traveled from university to university and studied mathematics, geography, astronomy, and as much as he could about the heavens. He observed very closely the movement of the sun, the planets, and the stars. Like certain ancient Greeks, he believed that the earth and the planets went around the sun.

After studying the movements of the sun, the planets, and the stars for a long time, he told other people that the earth goes around the sun. They did not believe him. They said, "If you are right, then why does the sun rise in the east and set in the west?"

Copernicus replied, "Because the earth spins like a top, and the sun stands still. It only seems that the sun is moving."

Copernicus explained his ideas in books for everyone to read, but people still would not believe him.

Another very wise man named Galileo helped prove that this new idea was right. He improved the telescope, so that at last people could see the sun, the planets, and the moon much better. He was the first man to see the moons circling around Jupiter and many other interesting things. He wrote a book about his new discoveries. He explained why Copernicus was right, even though many people still thought the sun went around the earth.

Today we have bigger and better telescopes to look at the stars, and we know that Copernicus and Galileo were right. These men were great men because they believed what they observed instead of what other people said. They did not discover a new world on earth as Columbus did, but they learned many things about other worlds in the sky that nobody had known about before.

Today, even though we know that the earth moves around the sun, we still talk about the sunrise and the sunset.

QUESTIONS

1. Why does the sun seem to be moving around the earth?
2. What did Copernicus try to show in his book?
3. Why could Galileo find out more than Copernicus about the sun, the planets, and the moon?
4. Why were Copernicus and Galileo great men?
5. Find out who Johannes Kepler was and what he did.
6. Who was Sir Isaac Newton?
7. Find out more about the movement of the earth, the moon, and the planets.
8. What is a solar system? A galaxy?

THE MOON

People have always liked to look up at the moon on a clear night. When the moon is full, sometimes it looks like a giant lantern that lights the night sky. Sometimes there seems to be a person in the moon looking down on us, and sometimes there seems to be a witch or a donkey in the moon.

Since olden times, people have sung songs and told many different legends about the moon, for it was the most popular of all the heavenly bodies. Above all, people have wondered at its beauty and wondered why it is forever changing. They thought that these changes had something to do with the birth, growth, death, and rebirth of many things on Earth. That is why people of olden times were careful to see whether the moon was in the right spot in the sky before they were going to do something important. They wanted the moon to bring them good luck.

Long ago people did not have calendars, but they wanted to count the days in some way. They noticed that about once every twenty-eight days there was a *new* moon, so they called this length of time a *moonth*. In some places a man would blow a trumpet when he first sighted the *new* moon so that everyone would know a new *moonth* (or month) had begun.

WORDS TO WATCH

Soviet	*Eagle*	manned spacecraft
calendar	orbit	Honolulu
Tranquility Base	moon rocks	telescope
mankind	rebirth	heavenly bodies

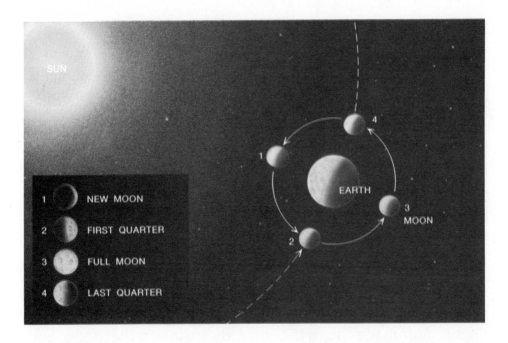

In the last few hundred years, people have looked at the moon through telescopes and learned more about it than ever before. We know that the moon is not changing its shape each night, as people used to think, but that it is traveling around the earth, and that the sunlight shines on it a little differently each night.

It is a *new* moon when the moon is between the earth and the sun so that we can hardly see the side that the sun is shining on. It is a *full* moon when the moon moves to the other side of the earth. Then the moon is on one side of the earth, and the sun on the other side so that we can see all of the moon that the sun is shining on.

Because of the way in which the earth and moon move, one side of the moon always faces earth. Until 1959 when a Soviet spacecraft traveled around the moon and took pictures, no one knew what the other side looked like. Since then, men too have traveled around the moon.

On Sunday, July 20, 1969, one of humanity's oldest dreams came true. On that day at 4:17 p.m. Eastern Daylight Time, Neil Armstrong and Edwin (Buzz) Aldrin safely landed America's manned spacecraft *Eagle* on the moon. Eight hundred million people were thrilled to hear Neil Armstrong's now-famous words: "Tranquility Base here. The *Eagle* has landed." And 800 million people watched, by television, one of the most exciting adventures in history; the first human step onto the surface of the moon. No one who watched will ever forget the moment when Neil Armstrong's ghostly white figure appeared outside *Eagle,* when his heavy-booted foot made the first human footprint on the moon, and when his voice was heard once again, "That's one small step for man, one giant leap for mankind."

After two hours and twenty minutes of exploring and gathering moon rocks, the men climbed back into *Eagle*. They guided their spacecraft back to the waiting mother ship *Columbia* in which Michael Collins, the third man of the team, had orbited the moon. Together they returned to earth exactly as planned, splashing down 950 miles west of Honolulu on July 24.

When we look up at the moon now, it somehow does not seem so far away and strange any more. We know that somewhere on its surface stands our flag and, not far from it, on the historic landing spot, a plaque signed by the astronauts and President Nixon which reads:

HERE MEN FROM THE PLANET EARTH FIRST SET FOOT UPON THE

MOON JULY 1969, A.D. WE CAME IN PEACE FOR ALL MANKIND

The Man in the Moon

Anonymous

The Man in the Moon, as he sails the sky,
Is a very remarkable skipper.
But he made a mistake
When he tried to take
A drink of milk from the Dipper.
He dipped right into the Milky Way
And slowly and carefully filled it.
The Big Bear growled
And the Little Bear howled,
And frightened him so, he spilled it.

The Nine Wanderers

The word *planet* comes from the Greek language, and it means "wanderer." At night, when the people of long ago looked up into the sky, they noticed that these planets had wandered to a new spot. They could see five of them with their naked eyes, and they named them after their gods.

These five planets that were known long ago are Mercury, Venus, Mars, Jupiter, and Saturn. Most people did not know where these planets wandered. Then, hundreds of years later,

---

WORDS TO WATCH

Mercury	Uranus	planet
Venus	Neptune	god
Mars	Pluto	goddess
Jupiter	Saturn	telescope
Copernicus	sun	North Pole
Galileo	moon	Earth

Copernicus and Galileo proved that they wandered around the sun. They knew that Earth was a planet and that it also wandered around the sun. That made six planets.

Later, three more planets were discovered. They were also given the names of the ancient people's gods: Uranus, Neptune, and Pluto. Today we know that there are at least nine planets all traveling around the sun, and that Earth is one of them.

The sun and the stars are like giant fireballs with giant flames leaping out from them. But planets are not like fireballs.

The smallest planet is Mercury. Because it appears to travel faster than the other planets it was named for the god that carried messages swiftly. It travels closer to the sun than any other planet.

Venus was named for the goddess of beauty. At night it shines brighter than any star in the sky. It is called the Evening Star when it shines in the western sky after the sun sets. And it is called the Morning Star when it shines in the eastern sky just before the sun rises.

Mars was named for the god of war. It looks like a red star in the sky. If you look at Mars through a telescope, you can see that it has poles with white caps, like the North Pole and the South Pole of our earth. Of all the planets besides Earth, Mars has an environment that seems most likely to be able to support forms of life.

Jupiter was king of the gods, and the planet named Jupiter is the largest of all the planets. More than one thousand planets the size of Earth could fit into Jupiter if it were hollow inside. There is only one moon that goes around the earth, but twelve moons go around Jupiter.

Saturn looks different from other planets because it has rings around it. Our earth takes only one year to travel around the sun. But Saturn takes about thirty of our years to go completely around the sun. If you lived on Saturn, you would have to wait about thirty years before you could have a birthday.

Uranus, Neptune, and Pluto are so far away that you cannot see them without a telescope. People did not know about these planets before the telescope was invented. Nobody can live on these planets because the temperature is much too cold. On Pluto you would have a birthday only once in every 248 years.

The more you learn about other planets, the happier you will be that you live on this one.

QUESTIONS

1. Why are planets thought of as "wanderers"?
2. How many planets are there? Name them.
3. Which planets did the ancient Greeks know about?
4. Which planet besides Earth is most likely to support life?
5. Read and spell the names of the planets listed on the next page and tell what you know about each planet.

Astronomy

I. Read and Spell

sun	moon	star
planet	Earth	Mercury
Venus	Mars	satellite
cosmic ray	Neptune	observatory
Saturn	meteor	galaxy
Pluto	telescope	Jupiter
the Milky Way	the Big Dipper	comet
North Star	constellation	the Little Dipper
light year	Orion	eclipse

II. Find Out and Answer

1. Find out about one of these, and tell the class about it.
2. What is the difference between a star and a planet?
3. What is the difference between a comet and a meteor?
4. Why do you think astronomy is important?

III. Write

1. Write a story about why you like to see the stars at night.
2. Write a story about a subject listed in Part I.

Stopping by Woods on a Snowy Evening

Robert Frost

Whose woods these are I think I know.
His house is in the village though;
He will not see me stopping here
To watch his woods fill up with snow.

My little horse must think it queer
To stop without a farmhouse near
Between the woods and frozen lake
The darkest evening of the year.

He gives his harness bells a shake
To ask if there is some mistake.
The only other sound's the sweep
Of easy wind and downy flake.

The woods are lovely, dark and deep.
But I have promises to keep,
And miles to go before I sleep,
And miles to go before I sleep.

QUESTIONS

1. Why did the driver stop his horse?
2. How does this poem help explain the difference between a man and a horse?

Marie Curie

Anonymous

Today scientists use modern equipment in their work. Special tools help scientists to find new things and to learn new facts.

In 1898, Marie Curie used huge iron kettles to melt tons of ore. Her work took four long years. At the end of all that time, she had a few grains of something that looked like table salt, but glowed in the dark. Yet those few grains gave doctors a way of saving the lives of thousands of people suffering from cancer. Studying them led to atomic power.

Marie Curie's long search began while she was studying in Paris, France. She read that uranium compounds had been found to give off strange rays. Scientists could not explain what these rays were. The rays acted something like X-rays. They could not be seen, but they left marks on camera film.

Marie wanted to learn more about the strange rays. Her husband, Pierre Curie, who taught physics, said that he

---

WORDS TO WATCH

Marie Curie	compound	ore
radium	Pierre Curie	element
uranium	Nobel Prize	physics
radioactive	thorium	Irène
exposed	diseased	chemicals

would like to help her on this project. They both wanted to solve the mystery of the rays.

They had very little money, so they could not afford a real laboratory. But a school agreed to let Marie use an old shed. The roof leaked. The shed was full of machinery and lumber, but there was room for the equipment she needed. She started to work.

She knew that uranium compounds gave off rays all the time. The rays never stopped. Marie tried using light and heat on these compounds. She mixed them with other chemicals. But nothing stopped or changed the rays. Pierre invented a machine that Marie used to measure the strength of the rays.

Uranium is an element. Elements are the simplest forms of matter. Iron, gold, and lead are elements. Two or more elements go together to make compounds. Salt, sugar, and rust are compounds. Scientists had found 80 elements in 1896. Marie wondered if any other elements had the power to send out these rays.

Patiently Marie tested every element known, either by itself or as a compound. Only thorium compounds gave off rays the way uranium compounds did.

Marie made up a new word—*radioactive*—to describe the chemicals that gave off rays all the time. And she called the rays *radioactivity*.

She decided to test minerals and ores. At first she found what she expected. Only those ores that contained uranium or thorium gave off the rays. If the ores contained a lot of uranium, they gave off many rays. If they had only a little uranium, they gave off only a few rays.

One day, Marie found an ore that gave off many rays. She measured the uranium in it. There was only a small amount. She thought that she made a mistake. But when she did the test over, she knew she was right. The ore gave off more rays than it would if the uranium were the only radioactive element in it. There could be only one answer. Some unknown element, one that was far more radioactive than uranium, had to be in the ore.

She wrote about her discovery. Some scientists agreed that there must be a new element they didn't know about. Other scientists didn't believe her. They said they knew exactly what elements were in the rocks. If there was another element there, Marie would have to show it to them.

Marie said that she would. Pierre was so excited that he gave up his own studies to work only with Marie.

They knew that the element would be very hard to find, because it had never been found before. They knew there was very little of it in the ore, so they would need a lot of ore. Uranium ore was very expensive, and they did not have enough money to buy all they needed.

One day they realized that the element they were looking for must still be in the ore after the uranium had been taken out. The used ore was just dumped in piles, because nothing could be done with it. The Curies were given a ton of the used ore for their work.

When the big sacks of ore arrived they were piled in the yard outside the shed. There was no room inside for the huge iron pots needed to melt it, so they were put outside too. Marie stood in the yard stirring the melting ore with a large

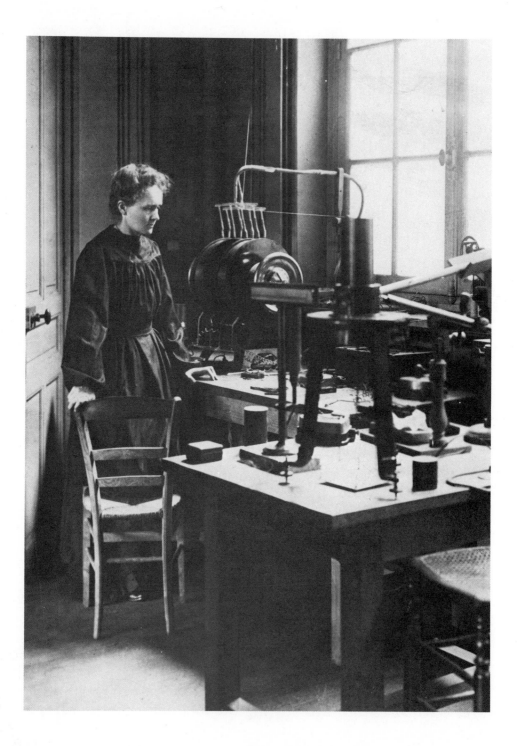

iron rod. After the ore melted, Marie added other chemicals that helped her find the new element.

For months Marie and her husband worked. They got more ore. They borrowed some money and got more equipment. After four years of hard work in the leaky shed, Pierre became sick. He had to give up for a while. Marie worked on alone.

In 1902, she succeeded. In the bottom of a test tube were a few tiny grains containing an element no one had ever seen before. Marie named the element radium.

It was an amazing element. It was five million times more radioactive than uranium. The rays could pass through wood and even steel. Only a thick screen of lead could block them.

They could act on a person's body. Marie's fingers had been badly burned by them. Pierre had purposely exposed himself to the rays, to see what would happen.

When doctors heard of these new rays, they wondered whether the rays could destroy diseased cells in the human body. They tried and found that the rays could. And after the diseased cells were destroyed, healthy cells often grew in their place. Because the rays worked this way, they could be used to treat some kinds of cancer.

At once, radium was wanted all around the world. Only the Curies knew how to get it out of the ore. The secret belonged to them. They could sell the secret in countries everywhere. They could become rich.

A letter came from America. People wanted to produce radium there. Pierre asked Marie what she wanted to do. Did she want to sell their secret, or did she want to give it away free?

"We did our work so scientists would have more knowledge," Marie said. "It would be wrong to sell what we know."

Pierre nodded. "You're right," he said. "I'll write back tonight and tell them everything they want to know."

Although the Curies chose not to profit from their work, they could not avoid fame. News of their discovery went everywhere. When she and Pierre were awarded the Nobel Prize in 1903, Marie Curie became world famous. When Pierre died in 1906, Marie was asked to take Pierre's place as a teacher. It was the first time that a woman had held this job.

Marie still worked on the radium compounds. She wanted to take radium out of the compounds and see it by itself. In 1910, she succeeded. Again she had done something so important that the news went everywhere. And in 1911 she was awarded another Nobel Prize. She was the first person to receive this famous award twice.

In 1921, Marie Curie visited the United States. She was asked what gift she would like most. Her reply was, "A gram of radium that would be mine to use." So the women of the United States raised $100,000 and bought a gram of radium. They gave it to Marie Curie.

Marie died in 1934, just one year before her daughter Irène was to receive a Nobel Prize. Irène had gone on with her mother's work on radioactive chemicals.

Robinson Crusoe

Adapted from Daniel Defoe

Robinson Crusoe was an English sailor who loved the sea. One time as he was sailing near South America, his ship struck a reef during a storm and was shipwrecked. The sailors climbed into a lifeboat, but that was soon dashed to pieces on the rocks. Everyone was drowned except Robinson Crusoe, who was luckily washed to the shore of a deserted island. There was no one to help him find food or shelter, and there was no way to leave the island.

But Robinson Crusoe knew how to do things for himself. He swam out to the broken ship, which was stuck in shallow

WORDS TO WATCH		
Robinson Crusoe	shelter	barley
South America	ammunition	diary
reef	crew	Bible
ashore	lumber	savages
island	racks	cannibals

133

water. From the ship he took food, guns, ammunition, water, clothes, tools, sailcloth, and lumber. Then he built a crude raft and returned to the island. He was able to make twelve trips to the ship before another storm destroyed it.

With the sailcloth he made a tent on the side of a small hill. Then he built a fence with sharp-pointed stakes to protect himself against enemies that might come to the island. He did not have much food, but with his guns he killed birds and small animals which he could cook and eat. He also found several springs on the island which gave him all the water he needed.

After a while, he made a bigger and stronger shelter in a cave that he found near the tent. The cave protected him from bad weather. He built shelves and racks for his guns, and he built a table and a chair.

He was able to grow corn and rice and barley so that he could make bread. He carefully saved the new kernels so that he could plant more grain the next year. He also found some wild goats on the island. He tamed the goats, and they gave him all the milk and meat he could eat.

On the ship he had found a pen and some ink, and he kept a diary of what he did every day. The diary also helped him keep track of the days and months and years. He also had found three Bibles on the ship, and he read them carefully. Every day he thanked God for all that he had.

One day he took a walk along the shore of the island. Suddenly he saw some strange footprints in the sand, and he became frightened. Someone else must be on the island! He went back to his shelter and prepared for an attack, but no one came. He searched the island, and he could find no one.

Some time later as he was looking around the island, he found many bones lying on the sand. They were human bones! Robinson saw where a fire had been made, but the men who had made it had left.

Robinson Crusoe lived alone on this island for twenty-four years. Many times he felt lonely, and he wanted someone to talk to, but no one came to visit him.

Then one time Robinson saw on the beach a group of savages from another island. They were cannibals who were preparing to eat their prisoners.

When Robinson Crusoe saw what was happening, he shot some of the cannibals, and the rest ran away. He was able to rescue one of the prisoners, and they became friends. Now Robinson Crusoe had someone to talk to. He called his new friend Friday because Friday was the day on which he had found him. He taught Friday to speak English, and Friday became his faithful companion.

Four years later, a ship passed near the island, and Robinson Crusoe and Friday were rescued. Together they sailed back to Robinson Crusoe's home in England.

The Umbrella

Two sages of Chelm went out for a walk. One carried an umbrella, the other didn't. Suddenly, it began to rain.

"Open your umbrella, quick!" suggested the one without an umbrella.

"It won't help," answered the other.

"What do you mean, it won't help? It will protect us from the rain."

"It's no use, the umbrella is as full of holes as a sieve."

"Then why did you take it along in the first place?"

"I didn't think it would rain."

Important Inventions

I. Read and Pronounce

wheel	rocket	radar
alphabet	airplane	gunpowder
printing press	automobile	compass
telephone	camera	electric motor
radio	steam engine	telescope
telegraph	gasoline engine	microscope
phonograph	electric light	typewriter
television	motion pictures	thermometer

II. Find Out and Answer

1. Why do you think each of these inventions is important?
2. Find out who invented these things:

    the radio   the steam engine   the electric light

3. Name some other important inventions.
4. Why do people say, "Necessity is the mother of invention"?

III. Write

Write a little story about an invention and why you think it is important.

I. A. You have read these stories about science and nature in Part Three of your book. Write or tell what each story is about.

    The Wonderful Alphabet
    The Invention of Printing
    Copernicus and Galileo
    The Moon
    The Nine Wanderers
    Marie Curie
    Robinson Crusoe

    B. Write or tell the class which story you liked best and why you liked it.

II. A. Write or tell the class which story you like best in the whole book and why you like it.

    B. Which poem did you like best in the whole book? Why?

III. A. Memorize a poem in this book and recite it to your class.

    B. Write a short poem of your own.

Part Four

For Readers
Brave and Bold

The Night Before Christmas

Clement C. Moore

'Twas the night before Christmas, when all through the house
Not a creature was stirring, not even a mouse;
The stockings were hung by the chimney with care,
In hopes that St. Nicholas soon would be there.
The children were nestled all snug in their beds,
While visions of sugar-plums danced in their heads;
And Mamma in her 'kerchief, and I in my cap,
Had just settled our brains for a long winter's nap,
When out on the lawn there arose such a clatter,
I sprang from my bed to see what was the matter.
Away to the window I flew like a flash,
Tore open the shutters and threw up the sash.
The moon on the breast of the new-fallen snow
Gave the luster of midday to objects below,
When, what to my wondering eyes should appear,
But a miniature sleigh, and eight tiny reindeer,
With a little old driver, so lively and quick,
I knew in a moment it must be St. Nick.
More rapid than eagles his coursers they came,
And he whistled, and shouted, and called them by name,
"Now, Dasher! Now, Dancer! Now, Prancer and Vixen!
On Comet! On, Cupid! On, Donder and Blitzen!
To the top of the porch! To the top of the wall!
Now dash away! Dash away! Dash away all!"
As dry leaves that before the wild hurricane fly,
When they meet with an obstacle, mount to the sky,

So up to the housetop the coursers they flew
With the sleigh full of toys, and St. Nicholas, too.
And then, in a twinkling, I heard on the roof
The prancing and pawing of each little hoof.
As I drew in my head, and was turning around,
Down the chimney St. Nicholas came with a bound.
He was dressed all in fur, from his head to his foot,
And his clothes were all covered with ashes and soot;
A bundle of toys he had flung on his back,
And he looked like a peddler just opening his pack.
His eyes—how they twinkled! His dimples how merry!
His cheeks were like roses, his nose like a cherry!
His droll little mouth was drawn up like a bow,
And the beard on his chin was as white as the snow;
The stump of a pipe he held tight in his teeth,
And the smoke it encircled his head like a wreath;
He had a broad face and a little round belly
That shook, when he laughed, like a bowlful of jelly.
He was chubby and plump, a right jolly old elf,
And I laughed when I saw him, in spite of myself;
A wink of his eye and a twist of his head
Soon gave me to know I had nothing to dread;
He spoke not a word, but went straight to his work,
And filled all the stockings; then turned with a jerk,
And laying his finger aside of his nose
And giving a nod, up the chimney he rose;
He sprang to his sleigh, to his team gave a whistle
And away they all flew like the down of a thistle.
But I heard him exclaim, ere he drove out of sight,
"Happy Christmas to all, and to all a good night."

Winter in the Mountains

Johanna Spyri

Suddenly a lot of snow fell during the night, and in the morning the whole meadow was white with snow. Not one single green leaf could be seen anywhere. Heidi was amazed as she looked through the little window, for now it started to snow again, and the heavy flakes fell on and on, until the snow was so high that it reached up to the window and then still higher so that you could not even open the window.

Heidi thought this was so funny. She ran from one window to the other, wondering whether the snow might soon cover the whole hut so that they would need to light candles in the middle of the day. Finally it stopped snowing, and the next day Grandfather went outside and shoveled around the whole house, making big piles of snow. The hut looked as if it were surrounded by snow-capped mountains. The windows and the door were cleared once again, and this was good, for in the afternoon a visitor was coming.

143

Heidi and Grandfather were sitting by the fire, when all of a sudden they heard a loud thumping and something rapping against the door again and again. Finally the door opened, and in came Peter. It was not out of naughtiness that he had rapped against the door, but to get the snow off his boots, which were still all covered. All of Peter was covered with snow, because he had to battle through high drifts on his way up. In the bitter cold, big chunks of snow had frozen onto his coat and pants. But he did not give up. Today he wanted to visit Heidi, whom he had not seen for a whole week.

"Good evening," he said as he came in, and he stood by the fire as closely as possible, not saying another word. His whole face beamed with pleasure that he was there. Heidi looked at him in amazement, for as he was now so close to the fire, everything on him started to thaw, so that all of Peter looked like a small waterfall.

Grandfather got up and brought the supper out of the cupboard, and Heidi moved the chairs to the table. Peter opened his round eyes wide when he saw the big piece of good dried meat which Grandfather put on his thick slice of bread. Peter had not had it so good for a long time.

When the cheerful meal was over, it started to get dark and Peter had to think of going home. He said "Good night" and "God thank you" and was already outside when he came back once more. "Next Sunday I'll be back again, a week from today," he said. "And my Grandmother told me that you should come and visit her sometimes."

Now this was a completely new idea for Heidi, that she should visit someone. But she liked the idea very much, and

the very next morning Heidi's first words were, "Grandfather, now I surely will have to go down to Grandmother;
she is expecting me."

"There is too much snow," Grandfather replied. But Heidi
was determined to go, because Grandmother had given her
the message to come, so it had to be. She had to do it. Not a
single day passed but that Heidi would say five or six times,
"Grandfather, now I will have to go for sure; Grandmother is
waiting for me!"

On the fourth day when it was so cold outside that every
step creaked and crunched and the whole big blanket of snow
all around was frozen hard, the beautiful sun peeked into the
window just onto Heidi's big chair, where she was eating her
lunch. Then she started her little story again. "Today I really
have to go to see Grandmother. Otherwise she just will have
to wait too long." Then Grandfather got up, climbed up into
the hayloft, brought down the heavy sack which was Heidi's
blanket, and said, "So come now!"

Heidi jumped for joy and skipped out after him into the
sparkling snow. Now it was very quiet in the old fir trees. The
white snow covered all their branches, and all trees glittered
and sparkled in such splendor that Heidi jumped with delight
and shouted again and again, "Come out, Grandfather, come
out! There is nothing but silver and gold on the fir trees!"

Grandfather had gone into the shed and now came out with
a wide sled: it had a board fastened to one side, and you could
sit on the sled. Putting down your legs on both sides, you
could steer it by dragging your feet in the snow. Grandfather
sat down on it, after Heidi and he had looked at the glistening

fir trees all around. He took the child on his lap, wrapped the heavy blanket around her so that she would be nice and warm, and held her closely with his left arm. This was necessary for the coming trip. Then he held onto the sled with his right hand and gave a jerk with both his feet. Right away the sled shot down the mountain with such speed that Heidi thought she was flying in the air like a bird, and she shouted loudly for joy.

All of a sudden the sled came to a stop just in front of Peter's hut. Grandfather lifted Heidi off the sled, unwrapped the blanket, and said, "Now, go inside, and when it begins to get dark, come out again and start back home!" Then he turned around with his sled and pulled it back up the mountain.

This story is from a book called *Heidi* written by Johanna Spyri. Heidi had a quiet and happy life with Grandfather on the mountain, but something happened to change her life. You can read more about Heidi if you borrow the book from your library.

QUESTIONS
---

1. Why was Heidi amazed when she looked out of the window of the hut?
2. What happened after it stopped snowing?
3. What did the visitor look like, and why did he come?
4. Did Heidi like the invitation? Why?
5. How did the fir trees look in the sunshine?
6. Tell how Heidi and Grandfather got down the mountain.

The Dead Tree

Alvin Tresselt

It stood tall in the forest. For a hundred years or more, the oak tree had grown and spread its shade. Birds nested in its shelter. Squirrels made their homes in bundles of sticks and leaves held high in the branches. And in the fall they stored their winter food from acorns that fell from the tree.

Tucked under its roots, small creatures were safe from the fox and the owl. Slowly, slowly, over the years the forest soil grew deeper as the dry brown leaves, brought down by the autumn winds, decayed under the snow.

But even as the tree grew, life gnawed at its heart. Carpenter ants tunneled through the strong oak. Termites ate out hallways from top to bottom. A broken limb let a fungus enter the heartwood of the tree. A rot spread inside the healthy bark.

Year by year, the tree grew weaker as its enemies worked inside it. Each spring fewer and fewer leaves unfolded. Its great branches began to turn gray with death. Woodpeckers covered the limbs with holes, looking for the tasty grubs and beetles that had tunneled the wood. Here and there they dug bigger holes to hold their babies.

In winter storms, one by one, the great branches broke and crashed to the floor of the forest. Then there remained only the proud trunk holding its broken arms up to the sky.

Now it was the autumn weather. The days were long and lazy. Yellow-gray and misty mornings, middays filled with false summer warmth, and sharp frosty nights.

Then came a day of high wind and slashing rain. As the fierce wind shrieked through the forest, the tree split off and crashed to the ground. There it lay in pieces, with only a jagged stump to mark where it had stood for so long.

The cruel days of winter followed. A family of deer mice settled into a hole that had once held a long branch. A rabbit found shelter from the cold wind in the rotted center of the trunk. The ants and termites, the sleeping grubs and fungus waited out the winter weather, under the bark and deep in the wood.

In the spring the sun warmed the forest floor. Last year's acorns sprouted to replace the fallen giant. Now new life took over the dead tree.

Old woodpecker holes made snug homes for chipmunks. A family of raccoons lived in the hollow center of the trunk. Under the bark, the wood-eating fungus spread a ghostlike

and sulphur-yellow coat. And deep inside, the carpenter ants and the termites continued their digging and eating.

On the underside, where the trunk lay half buried in the damp leaf loam, the mosses formed a soft green carpet. Fragile ferns clustered in its shadow. Mushrooms popped up out of the decaying mold. Scarlet clumps of British soldiers sprinkled the loose bark.

The years passed. The oak's hard wood grew soft. A hundred thousand grubs and beetles crawled through it. Many-legged centipedes, snails, and slugs fed on the rotting wood. And earthworms made their way through the feast. All these creatures helped to turn the tree once more into earth.

Pale shelf fungus grew on the stump like giant clamshells, eating away and growing as the tree decayed.

A skunk came by with her babies. Sniffing at the wood, she ripped into the softness to uncover the scrambling life inside.

Eagerly the skunk family feasted. Quiet forest birds scratched and picked for grubs and worms, pulling the tree apart bit by bit. The melting winter snows and soft spring rains helped to speed the rotting of the wood.

In this way, the great oak returned to the earth. There remained only a brown ghost of richer loam on the ground where the proud tree had come to rest. And new trees grew in strength from acorns that had fallen long years ago.

QUESTIONS

1. What did the *living* oak tree provide for other living things? How?
2. What did the *dead* oak tree provide for other living things? How?
3. Why was the dead, decaying tree as important to nature as the living tree?

The Judgment of Solomon

The Bible

A long time ago a great king named Solomon ruled over Israel. When he first became king, God appeared to him in a dream and said, "Solomon, you are a good man. What gift would you like most to have?"

"I would like most of all the gift of wisdom to rule my people well," said Solomon.

God was pleased that Solomon asked for great wisdom rather than great wealth or great power, and he said to Solomon, "You shall be wiser than any man on earth, and you shall be richer than any other king."

WORDS TO WATCH		
Solomon	wisdom	Israel
ruled	complaints	judgment
spare		sword

In those days kings often listened to the complaints of their people, and then the kings would judge who was right and who was wrong. One day two women came before Solomon. They told Solomon that they both lived in the same house. Each of them had a very young child. In the night one of the children died. The mother took her dead child and put it in the bed where the living child was sleeping and took the living child away with her.

When morning came the other awoke and saw what had happened. She tried to get her living child back, but the woman who had stolen it would not give it back. So both women went before King Solomon, and each said that the living child was hers.

Solomon had to decide who was the real mother. He ordered a servant to bring him a sword. Then he ordered some other servants to cut the living child in two with the sword and give each woman half.

The woman who stole the child did not object to this plan. But the real mother of the child cried out, "Give the child to this woman, but spare its life!"

Then the wise Solomon knew that the mother who cried out was the real mother. He knew that she loved the child so much that she would rather give it to the other woman than to see it killed.

Solomon said to the servants, "Give the child to her, for she is the real mother."

When the people of Israel heard about this judgment of Solomon, they knew that he was the wisest of men.

1. When God asked Solomon what gift he would most like to have, what did Solomon ask for?
2. Why was God pleased with Solomon's answer?
3. What did one of the mothers do that was bad?
4. How did Solomon decide who was the real mother?
5. Why was this judgment of Solomon a wise judgment?

Puss-in-Boots

Charles Perrault

There was once an old miller who had three sons. When the old miller died, he had nothing to give to his sons except his mill, his donkey, and his cat. The oldest son took the mill, the second son took the donkey, and the youngest son had to take the cat.

This made the youngest son feel very sad. "What am I to do?" he said. "My oldest brother can grind wheat with his windmill, and my other brother can carry sacks of flour from the mill on his donkey. But what can I do with a cat? I can eat him and sell his skin, but then what will I do? I shall die of hunger."

WORDS TO WATCH

miller	mowers	ogre
reapers	Marquis of Carabas	partridges

The cat heard these words and looked up at his master. "Do not worry," he said. "You will not have to eat me. Only give me a bag and get me a pair of boots, and I will show you how we can live very well."

The young man did not see how the cat could help him to live, but he knew the cat was clever. Besides, what else could the young man do?

So he got the cat a bag and a pair of boots. Puss put on the boots and tied the bag around his neck. Then he set off for a place where there were some rabbits.

He filled the bag with grain and left the mouth of the bag open. Then he lay down and pretended to go to sleep. Soon a young rabbit smelled the grain and saw the open bag. He crawled into the bag to eat the grain. Quickly the cat drew the strings of the bag closed and caught the rabbit.

Puss now went to the palace and asked to speak to the king. The guards took him to the king. He made a low bow and said, "Sire, this is a rabbit which my master asked me to give to you."

"And who is your master?" said the king.

"He is the Marquis of Carabas," said the cat, bowing low.

"Tell your master that I gladly accept his gift," said the king with a smile. "Here are some coins for your master to show him that I like his gift. And before you go, get something for yourself in my kitchen."

Puss returned home and gave the coins to his master and said, "Now you need not go to bed hungry or sleep on the ground. And I have something else for you too."

"What can that be?" said the young man, amazed.

"A new name," said the cat. "From now on you are to be the Marquis of Carabas."

The young man thought this very amusing, and he burst out laughing.

The next day Puss took his bag and hid himself in a cornfield. This time he caught two partridges and took them to the king. The king thanked him as before and gave him more money.

Many times Puss caught birds and small animals, and each time he took them to the king, and the king gave him more money. And so Puss and his master always had plenty to eat and a good place to live.

One day Puss heard that the king and his daughter were going to take a drive along the banks of the river. Quickly he ran home to his master and said, "Do just as I tell you, and your fortune will be made. You need only go and bathe in the river at a certain spot and leave the rest to me."

"Very well," said his master. He did as the cat told him, but he did not understand what Puss was going to do.

While he was bathing in the river, the king and the princess

drove by. Puss jumped out of the bushes and cried, "Help! Help! The Marquis of Carabas is drowning! Save him!" The king heard the cry and looked out of his carriage. Then he saw the cat that had brought him so many birds and animals. The king ordered his men to run and help the Marquis. When he was out of the river, Puss explained to the king what had happened.

"My master was bathing, and some robbers came and stole his clothes. I ran after them and cried 'Stop thief!' but they got away. My master swam out into the deep water and would have drowned if you had not saved him."

The king felt sorry for the Marquis, and he ordered his servants to bring back a fine suit of clothes for him. The servants brought back a new suit, and soon the Marquis was dressed more finely than he had ever been before in his life. He looked so handsome that the king invited him to ride in his carriage beside the princess.

Puss-in-Boots ran on in front of the carriage and soon came to a meadow. Some men were mowing grass. Puss came up to them and said, "I say, good folks, the king is coming this way. Be good enough to tell him that these fields belong to the Marquis of Carabas."

The mowers agreed.

Soon the king's carriage came down the road. The king stuck his head out and said, "This is good grassland. Who owns it?"

"The Marquis of Carabas, sire," they all said.

"You have a fine estate, Marquis," said the king to the young man.

"Yes, sire," replied the Marquis, "it pays me well."

Puss ran on farther and soon came upon some reapers who were cutting grain.

"I say," he cried, "the king is coming this way. If he asks whose grain this is, be good enough to tell him that it belongs to the Marquis of Carabas." The reapers agreed.

Soon the king came by, and when he asked the reapers who owned the grain, they replied, "The Marquis of Carabas, sire."

The new Marquis liked to pretend that he owned all this land and grain, and the king and princess were amazed.

Soon the carriage came toward a large castle. In this castle lived an ogre, and this ogre was the real owner of all the land the carriage had been passing through.

Again Puss-in-Boots ran on ahead of the carriage. He asked to speak to the ogre. A servant led Puss into a large room where the ogre was sitting. Puss stood a safe distance away and said, "I have heard that you can change yourself into any kind of animal you wish. But I do not believe that you can do it. Can you change yourself into a lion?"

"Of course I can change myself into a lion," roared the ogre. "Just watch me."

In no time at all the ogre became a lion, and now he roared louder than ever.

When Puss saw the ogre become a lion, he almost jumped out of his boots.

"Wonderful! Marvelous!" he exclaimed. "But I do not think that you can change yourself into a mouse, for a mouse is very small."

The ogre changed himself back into his own ugly shape and said, "Just watch me. I can become a mouse as easily as I can become a lion."

And quick as a wink the ogre became a mouse, and quicker than a wink the cat gobbled up the mouse. And that was the end of the ogre.

By now the king's carriage was in front of the castle. When Puss-in-Boots heard the noise of the carriage wheels, he ran outside and met the king at the gate.

"Welcome, your majesty, to the castle of my master, the Marquis of Carabas," he said.

"What!" said the king, turning to the young man. "Does this castle also belong to you? I have never seen such a fine castle."

They all went inside and found that a great feast was waiting for them. The cat invited them to sit down, and they all ate until they could eat no more.

After the meal Puss whispered in his master's ear, "This castle really does belong to you. When your grandfather lived, he was the true Marquis of Carabas. He was driven from his castle and his lands by an ogre, but I am happy to say that the ogre will harm you no more. It is right that you be called the Marquis of Carabas from now on. You are the true owner of this castle and these lands."

When the young man heard these words, he jumped for joy. Soon afterward he asked the princess to marry him, and the princess accepted. Now everybody was happy, including Puss-in-Boots, who did not run after mice any more except for fun.

QUESTIONS

1. What did Puss-in-Boots's master have at the beginning of the story? What did he have at the end of the story? Why did he have more at the end of the story?
2. What are some of the things Puss-in-Boots did that show he was clever?
3. Why did the castle really belong to Puss-in-Boots's master?
4. Do you feel sorry for the ogre? Why?

Doña Felisa

On Wednesday mornings the city hall in San Juan, Puerto Rico, became the house of the people. Every week on that day, the mayor of San Juan, Felisa Rincón de Gautier, held open house. Wearing one of the astonishing hats that were her trademark, she came into the council room where hundreds of people waited. She wished a good day to these people, her friends—"*Buenos días, amigos.*" They answered, "*Buenos días, Doña Felisa.*" Then she took her seat at a simple table. One by one the people came up for a few moments of quiet talk. She helped them to get whatever it was they needed—school shoes, medical care, or a place to live. Perhaps just comfort and advice were needed. She would not leave the room until she had talked with everyone there.

The story of how Doña Felisa became mayor of the capital city of Puerto Rico is partly a story of changing ideas about the place of women in public life.

Felisa was the eldest of eight children in a well-to-do family. When she was twelve years old, her mother died. After a time, her father decided that he needed his eldest daughter to run the household. So Felisa, who had hoped to become a

---

WORDS TO WATCH

San Juan	*barrios*	Felisa Rincón de Gautier
amigos	poverty	Puerto Rico
Doña	population	*buenos días*
trademark	Don Jenaro	political party
reform	open house	Luis Muñoz Marín

161

doctor, had to leave high school. It would have been very hard for a young girl, brought up in the old Spanish way, to argue with her father. Even about her own future.

Felisa went on being an obedient daughter. Her father decided that he would move his family to the country and spend only weekends with them. Although she missed the city, Felisa had to go to the country to take care of her younger brothers and sisters and to run the family farm. She became an able manager.

At last a time came when Felisa could no longer bow to every wish of her father. In 1917, Congress had passed a law making Puerto Ricans citizens of the United States. In 1920, it had passed another law giving women on the mainland the right to vote. After some years, Puerto Rico also gave women that right. Felisa wanted to register to vote, but her father objected. This time, however, she would not give in. She won her father's consent and was proud to be among the first women to sign the voting register.

When she registered to vote, she joined the political party of Luis Muñoz Marín. From that day on, Felisa made herself useful to her political party. Her special job was to bring the party's promise of reform to the poor people of San Juan. She made friends with the people who lived in the *barrios*—the slums. She saw that poverty and hunger were growing in Puerto Rico, along with the growth in population. Luis Muños Marín was to become the governor of Puerto Rico for many years. His famous "Operation Bootstrap" was a program to build the wealth and independence of Puerto Rico. Felisa was determined to do whatever she could to help.

After years of party work, Doña Felisa was well-known and loved in the city. Her party then asked her to run for mayor. Now it was her husband, Don Jenaro, who objected. Once again, she bowed to the wish of a man she loved. But she was not happy about it. When she had a second chance to become mayor, she accepted. This time Don Jenaro agreed.

Doña Felisa was elected then and many other times. She was mayor of San Juan for twenty-two years in all. During that time she cleaned up the city. She built a chain of nursery schools and improved the hospitals. She made sure that the poor children of the city had shoes and clothes and toys at Christmas. And she encouraged Puerto Rican women to be active in public life. But perhaps she is best remembered for her Wednesdays—those days when she held open house and the city hall became the house of the people.

QUESTIONS

1. What did Doña Felisa do on Wednesdays when she was mayor?
2. In what ways did Doña Felisa help the people of San Juan?
3. How long did Doña Felisa serve as mayor of San Juan?
4. On a map, find Puerto Rico and San Juan.

Ludwig van Beethoven: A Song in a Silent World

Wherever he went, Ludwig van Beethoven heard music. He heard music when the wind whispered through the leaves, or went sssshh-sssshh-sssshh across the grass, or roared from the sky to bend trees and break branches.

Music filled Ludwig's home, too. His father was a singer in the royal choir that sang in the palace of the Elector (a German prince). Ludwig's neighbors played many instruments and every night they gave a concert, singing and playing music that could be heard for miles, all the way up to the sky.

In fact, Ludwig's whole life was music. When he was four years old, he began taking piano lessons from his father. Soon he played the violin. Outdoors, his friends played hide-and-seek, but Ludwig's father kept him indoors, practicing. "You will be a great musician," his father said. "You will give concerts and bring us extra money."

There was never enough money in Ludwig's house. His father did not earn enough to feed Ludwig and his brothers and mother, or to buy wood for the fireplace and clothes for

---

WORDS TO WATCH

Ludwig van Beethoven		concertos
Elector	violin	symphonies
concert	viola	orchestra
Herr Pfeiffer	cello	quartets
musicians	chorale	Vienna

everyone to wear. Ludwig's mother sold their silver and even some of their furniture to get money for food.

So Ludwig knew he had to do something to help his family, and to fill his own empty stomach.

When he was seven, Ludwig gave his first concert in the palace where his father was a singer. All the seats were filled with rich people. Ludwig looked at their waiting faces, took a deep breath, put his strong fingers on the piano keys, and began to play.

"Bravo! Bravo!" shouted the audience when he finished. "Again! Again!" So Ludwig played again. His father was very proud. And Ludwig was given money by the Elector who lived in the palace.

But playing the piano and violin wasn't enough for Ludwig. There was different music inside his head. Sometimes it was so loud, it was all he could hear. He wanted to write it down, so a whole orchestra could play it.

Ludwig asked his new teacher, Herr (Mr.) Pfeiffer, to teach him to write music on paper. But as soon as Ludwig learned, he became so busy that he hardly had time to write any music.

Part of the time he was in school learning arithmetic and Latin. He practiced the piano, the violin, and now the organ, too, every day. He gave concerts at the palace. Soon he was playing the organ for church services every morning at six o'clock.

But Ludwig did write music, more and more each year. "I won't just play *other* people's music," he thought. "I want to write my own and play it. I want the whole world to be in my music."

And the whole world *was* in his music. Ludwig wrote music with thunderstorms, and music with dancing. Some of his music sounded like armies marching to war and fighting battles in ruined cities. Then his music sounded like funerals of men killed in fighting.

He wrote music for voices, for piano, for violin, for piano and violin together, for many violins, for whole orchestras. He tried every combination he could think of. He loved them all.

Soon Ludwig's music was played everywhere. He became

famous and moved to Vienna, a town filled with music-loving people and with musicians like himself.

He was grown up, but in many ways he was still a young boy, playing the piano all day and most of the night. His manners were rough, his clothes often untidy or dirty. But his wonderful music made him important friends—great musicians and great noblemen.

One day he heard a new sound—a strange sound. What was it? A buzzing, an odd buzzing in his ears. Ludwig frowned. The buzzing bothered the music in his head. He shook his head back and forth but the buzzing was still there.

The buzzing became such a roar that Ludwig was frightened. "I cannot hear my music!" he shouted. He went to his doctor. "My ears, my ears," he said. "And my music." He shook all over. He wanted to play music, but all he could hear was a buzzing and a roaring in his head.

The doctor looked into Ludwig's ears and held Ludwig's head and looked again into his ears. "Well?" said Ludwig. "Make the noise go away!"

Slowly, sadly, the doctor shook his head. "No, my friend," he said. "Your ears are sick. The noise will stay for a while. But when it does go away, you will not hear anything."

Ludwig stared at the doctor. *"Anything?"* he whispered.

"You will be deaf," said the doctor.

"But I can't be deaf!" shouted Ludwig. "I must hear my music!" He ran from the doctor's office. When he got home, he slammed the door and for days no one saw him. He sat in his room, his head in his hands, trying to think. "My music," he said. Again and again, "My music, my music."

But a strange thing happened. When the buzzing and roaring stopped, the music came back into Ludwig's head. The world was silent—he couldn't hear anything around him. He couldn't hear children shouting and people singing; he couldn't hear birds or the wind or the clatter of horses' hooves on the street. When people moved their lips, there were no voices for him to hear. But he heard all the music in his head.

He wrote and wrote. Eight symphonies for orchestra. Five concertos for piano and one for the violin. An opera. Sixteen quartets for chamber groups—two violins, a viola, and a cello. And hundreds of other works for all instruments.

One day Ludwig began a new symphony. When he came to the fourth part of the symphony (the fourth movement), the instruments were not enough for him. He added new "instruments"—people singing. The fourth movement of his symphony was a giant song. It was called the "Ode to Joy." He wrote it about friendship and joy in the world, no matter what problems people had, like his own deafness, or another person's blindness, or another's lameness, or even poverty or sickness.

The symphony was finished. Ludwig's friends played parts of it on the piano. Word of the symphony spread from town to town. "A great symphony," it was called. "So beautiful," people said. "No symphony like it has ever been heard." But some people hated it, because it was so huge and hard to play. It was called *The Chorale,* or Beethoven's Ninth. Later it was known simply as the Ninth, for no other symphony was like it.

From the time he finished the Ninth Symphony until the end of his life four years later, Beethoven was troubled by sickness and worry. He was completely deaf and very poor. But in those years he wrote some of his greatest music. He seemed to enter a new world where no one had ever been before. His music was like none ever written. And every composer who came after Beethoven has looked up to him and learned from him.

QUESTIONS

---

1. Would it be hard to compose music if you were deaf? Why or why not?
2. Vienna is often called "the city of music." Find out the names of three other great composers who lived there.
3. Find out the name of the city Beethoven was born in.

Rachel Carson

When Rachel Carson was a little girl growing up in a small town in Pennsylvania, her mother taught her to take pleasure in the outdoors and in birds, insects, and fish. Young Rachel's two loves were nature and writing. It was no surprise to those who knew her that she grew up to be a scientist and a writer about nature.

Above all, she came to love the sea. She wanted to learn about the different kinds of living things that swim in the oceans, fly above them, and move on their shores. She studied marine biology, and worked during the summers at the Woods Hole Marine Biological Laboratory on Cape Cod. Finally, she went to work for the U. S. Fish and Wildlife Service. Part of her job was to write about how to protect our country's birds, fish, and other forms of wildlife.

Then she began to write for the public. In her most famous book, *The Sea Around Us,* she tells of the gray beginnings of the sea and of its storms and tides. She writes about the many strange creatures that live in the sea. Her book was widely

---

WORDS TO WATCH

marine	eternal	balance of nature
biology	creatures	Marine Biological
public	environment	Laboratory
ebb	sprays	
marsh	generation	

enjoyed because she was able to make people understand both the science and poetry of the sea. In *The Sea Around Us,* she writes:

> To stand at the edge of the sea, to sense the ebb and flow of the tides, to feel the breath of a mist over a great salt marsh, to watch the flight of shore birds that have swept up and down the surf lines of the continents for untold thousands of years, . . . is to have knowledge of things that are as nearly eternal as any life can be.

Later, Rachel Carson's interest in living things and their environments made her turn to a new subject. She wrote a book called *Silent Spring,* which many people read and talked about. In this book she told how certain chemicals used to kill insects could be unhealthy for other living things—including people. She called the spring "silent" because already, in some places in America, the birds which used to sing in the springtime were not returning to their nests. Their insect food had been poisoned by sprays meant only to protect crops for people. The birds that did come back laid fewer eggs. The eggshells were thin and broke easily. She wrote about the *balance of nature*—the way in which all living things depend on one another. She showed how important it is not to upset this balance.

The ideas in *Silent Spring* were questioned by other scientists. These people knew that some chemicals upset the balance of nature. But they also knew that today's growing population could not live unless chemicals were used to kill harmful insects and weeds. They believed that they could find new ways to kill these pests.

Even though she was very shy, Rachel Carson defended her ideas with spirit. She started many people thinking about how important it was not to damage nature, which is very delicately balanced by many unseen and unknown forces. "I deeply believe that this generation must come to terms with nature," she said. Rachel Carson worked very hard to protect the lives of many of earth's creatures. Her efforts led many others to work for the same ends. Her success must have given Rachel Carson a deep feeling of joy as she went about her quiet life among her friends and pets, which were not fish and birds, as one might think, but cats.

QUESTIONS

1. Why are plants and animals important to human life?
2. What is your environment?
3. Find out more about the sea and some of the plants and animals that live in it.

Margaret Bourke-White

Helen Webber

Margaret Bourke-White was a photographer who could tell an exciting story in pictures. She was a pioneer in the art of photojournalism. Some pictures she took while lying in the snow and others while hanging out the door of an airplane. Some she took from the top of freight cars and some from the rafters of buildings. She photographed everything from the rural South to the frozen Arctic, from gold mining in South Africa to the bombing of Moscow in the Second World War. No conditions were too hard or dangerous for her to work under, no place too far away to travel to. People said of her, "Maggie won't take no for an answer."

Some of the picture-stories that Margaret Bourke-White liked best to tell were about industry. When she was a girl, she often went with her father, an absent-minded inventor, to visit factories. These trips were great adventures for her. She said later that the sudden magic of flowing metal and flying sparks had shaped her life's work. Yet photography was not her first idea for a career. In college she studied snakes and

---

WORDS TO WATCH		
photojournalism	torpedoed	fiery
rural	abilities	reptiles
studio	rafters	correspondent
industrial	career	crippling
furnace	factories	operation

Margaret Bourke-White photographing New York City (facing)

other reptiles. Not until she began taking pictures of the college and selling them to pay for her schooling did she think of photography as a career. In later years, she kept two pet alligators in her studio on the sixty-first floor of a New York skyscraper as a reminder of her earlier studies.

Margaret Bourke-White's industrial photographs were of factories, smoke stacks, bridges, water tanks, mines, and dams. This part of her work began at steel mills in Cleveland, Ohio, when she was a beautiful young woman of twenty-one. She had to show the factory owners that her strange desire to photograph a steel furnace was in fact a serious business. The first night that she was allowed to take pictures inside the steel mill was heaven to her. She was not dressed for the task. She had on a pretty dress and high-heeled shoes. And there she was, dancing on the edge of a fiery furnace, taking picture after picture and singing for joy. Later, Maggie learned to dress to suit her task, but she never stopped singing for joy.

Her later career took her to dozens of countries. She photographed famous leaders all over the world. She was a war correspondent and often went along on bombing flights. Once she was on a ship that was torpedoed, and all the passengers had to take to the lifeboats. Another time, the little airplane in which she was traveling had to land in heavy fog on a tiny island in the Arctic Ocean. And always she kept her cameras ready to record whatever adventure came her way. Her pictures were printed in magazines and collected in books. As time went on, she also wrote about her work and made speeches. She often said in her speeches that a photographer needed to be healthy and strong and able to do hard work.

Fort Peck Dam, Montana, 1936

South African gold miners, 1950 (facing)

Mahatma Gandhi, India, 1946

Steel worker and 200-ton ladle of molten steel, Otis Steel Mill (facing)

At the height of her powers, Margaret Bourke-White's health and strength failed her. A crippling illness struck her down and took from her the abilities she needed in her work.

But she was a fighter, and she fought back. After two brain operations and years of physical training, she was able to rise above her illness for a time. She took her usual keen interest in the war against her illness, and she allowed some of her photographer friends to record her progress in pictures. Margaret Bourke-White had once said, "I knew I would never run out of subjects that interested me while on this earth"—and she never did. She was a gifted and gallant woman who lived her life to the fullest.

QUESTIONS

1. If you were a photojournalist, what would you take pictures of ?
2. Why is taking pictures hard work?
3. Where would you keep a pet alligator?
4. Find out about other photojournalists.
5. Find out about the development of the camera and photography.

Glossary

a_, ă_	apple, tan		ea	eat, leap, tea
ā	acorn, table		_ĕa_	head, bread
à	alone, Donna		ee	eel, feet, see
â	air, care		er	herd, her
ä	father, wand		_ew	few, blew
ạ	all, ball		f	far, taffy, off
a_e	ape, bake		g	gas, wiggle, sag
ai_	aim, sail		ġ	gem, giant, gym
ȧr	calendar		gh_	ghost
är	art, park, car		_gh	though, thought (silent)
au_	author, Paul		h_	hat
aw	awful, lawn, saw		i_, ĭ_	it, sit
_ay	say, day		ī	pilot, pie
b	bat, able, tub		_ï_	babies, machine, *also*
c	cat, cot, cut			onion, savior, familiar
ce	cent, ace		i_e	ice, bite
ch	chest, church		_igh	high, bright
c̄h	chorus, ache		ir	irk, bird, fir
c̮h	chute		j_	jam
ci	cider, decide		k	kite, ankle, ink
_ci_	special		kn_	knife
_ck	tack, sick		l	lamp, wallet, tail
cy	bicycle		_le	table, ample
d	dad		m	man, bump, ham
_dge	edge, judge		_mb	lamb, comb
e_, ĕ_	elf, hen		n	no, tent, sun
ē	equal, me		_ñ_	uncle, anger
ė	moment, loaded		_ng	sing, ring

1. If a word ends in a silent *e,* as in **face,** the silent *e* is not marked. If a word ends in *-ed* pronounced **t,** as in **baked,** or **d,** as in **stayed,** no mark is needed. If the ending *-ed* forms a separate syllable pronounced **ėd,** as in **load'ėd,** the *e* has a dot.

2. If there are two or three vowels in the same syllable and only one is marked, as in **beaū'ty, friĕnd, rōgue,** or **breāk,** all the other vowels in the syllable are silent.

o_, ŏ_	odd, pot		_ti_	nation, station,
ō	go, no, toe			*also* question
ȯ	come, wagon		ṭu	congratulate
ô	off, song		u_, ŭ_	up, bus
oa_	oat, soap		ū	use, cute, *also*
o_e	ode, bone			granulate
oi_	oil, boil		ụ̄	truth, true
ŏŏ	book, nook		u̇	nature
o͞o	boot, zoo		ụ	pull, full
or	order, normal		ur	urge, turn, fur
ȯr	motor, doctor		ūr	cure, pure
ou_	out, hound		v	voice, save
ow	owl, town, cow		w_	will, wash
_ōw	low, throw		wh_	white, what
_oy	boy, toy		wr_	write
p	paper, tap		_x	extra, ax
ph	phone, elephant, graph		_x_	exist, example
qu_	quick, queen		y_	yes, yet
r	ram, born, ear		_y	baby, happy (when
s	sun, ask, yes			it is the only
_s̲	toes, hose			vowel in a final
_s̲_	vision, confusion			unstressed
ss̲	fission			syllable)
sh	show, bishop, fish		_y̆_	cymbal
t	tall, sets, bit		_ȳ	cry, sky
th	thick, three		ẏ	zephyr, martyr
th	this, feather, bathe		z	zoo, nozzle, buzz
_tch	itch, patch			

3. The Open Court diacritical marks in the Pronunciation Key make it possible to indicate the pronunciation of most unfamiliar words without respelling.

à·bil·i·ty *n.* The skill or power to do things.

Ac′crà *n.* The largest city and capital of Ghana.

Ac′ti·um *n.* A sea town in ancient Greece, site of the 31 B.C. naval battle between Octavian's fleet and the fleets of Mark Antony and Cleopatra.

A.D. The abbreviation for *anno Domini,* the Latin words meaning "in the year of our Lord," used with dates.

Af′ri·cà *n.* The second-largest continent.

Af′ri·càn *n.* A person who lives in or comes from Africa.

Al·ex·an′der III *n.* A king of ancient Greece who conquered most of the world known in his time (also known as Alexander the Great).

Al·ex·an′dri·à *n.* A city in Egypt at the mouth of the Nile River.

al′phà *n.* The first letter of the Greek alphabet.

Ält′dôrf *n.* A small town in Switzerland.

à·mï′gōs *n.* The Spanish word for "friends."

am·mū·nï′tïon *n.* Supplies for a gun, such as bullets and powder.

ăr′rànt *adj.* Downright; out-and-out; thorough.

Ā′șià Mī′nòr *n.* The peninsula bordered by the Black, Aegean, and Mediterranean seas.

às·ton′ish *v.* To surprise; to amaze.

Aus′tri·à *n.* A mountainous country of central Europe.

bal′ânce of nä′țùre The way that all living things depend on one another.

ban′ish *v.* To send away forcefully; to exile; to drive away.

ban′ner *n.* A flag; a pennant.

bär′lēy *n.* A kind of grain used for food.

bär′riôs *n.* The Spanish word for "slums."

bat′ter·ing ram *n.* A heavy device used to knock down gates, doors, and walls.

bawl *v.* To yell loudly; to cry continuously.

B.C. The abbreviation for "before Christ," used with dates.

Beethoven, Ludwig van (lud′wig van bā′tō·vėn) *n.* A German composer of music, especially known for his symphonies and sonatas.

bė·hĕad′ *v.* To cut off the head.

beta (bā′tà) *n.* The second letter of the Greek alphabet.

Bī′ble *n.* The scriptures of the Christian church; the Old and New Testaments.

Big Beâr *n.* Another name for the group of stars known as the Big Dipper.

bī·ol′ȯ·ġy *n.* The scientific study of life, both plant and animal.

black′bĕr·ry buck′le *n.* A kind of fruit dessert.

Bō·ad·ĭ·cē′à *n.* The queen of the Iceni, who led an uprising against the Roman rulers in Britain at the time of Nero.

bound *n.* A leap.

boy′cott *n.* An organized refusal to do business with.

brass *n.* A mixture of copper and zinc.

Brit′ain *n.* The old name for Great Britain, an island that lies just west of Europe.

British soldiers (brit′ish sōl′jers) *n.* A lichen that grows on dead trees or dry soil in the eastern United States, having a green stem and a red tip.

Bū·ceph′a·lus *n.* The horse used by Alexander the Great in most of his wars.

buenos días (bwā·nòs dē′às) The Spanish words for "good day," meaning "hello."

bur′nished *adj.* Polished.

but′ter·cup *n.* A wild plant with yellow, cup-shaped flowers.

bȳ′stand·er *n.* An onlooker; a spectator.

Cae′sar, Jul′ius *n.* A Roman general and statesman; the dictator of the Roman Empire from 49 to 44 B.C.

Cae·sâr′i·òn *n.* The son of Julius Caesar and Cleopatra.

cal′en·dar *n.* A system of dividing time into days, weeks, months, or years.

can′ni·bàl *n.* A man-eating savage.

cà·reer′ *n.* A profession.

cär′pen·ter ant *n.* Any of a group of large, black ants that build their nests in wood.

cast′ing on Putting yarn on a needle for knitting.

cat′a·pult *n.* A weapon once used to throw heavy objects at enemies.

Cath′o·lic *adj.* Of or belonging to the Roman Catholic church.

cello (chel′lō) *n.* A stringed musical instrument like a large violin with a deep tone.

cen′ti·pēde *n.* Any of a group of many-legged creatures that have two poisoned claws used to kill other insects.

cham′pi·òn *n.* An able and valiant fighter.

C̄helm *n.* A small town in Poland.

c̄hem′i·càl *n.* A substance, especially one whose reactions are studied by a chemist.

Chī·nēṣe′ *n.* The language of China.

c̄ho·răle′ *n.* A musical composition sung by a choir.

chunk *n.* A short, thick piece.

civ′il *adj.* Concerned with a nation; national.

Pronunciation Key

VOWELS: sat, hăve, āble, fäther, ạll, câre, ȧlone; yet, brĕad, mē, loadèd; it, practĭce, pīlot, machīne; hot, nō, ôff, wagòn; foŏt, foōd; oil, toy; count, town; up, ūse, trụth, pull; mȳth, baby, crȳ, zephȳr.

CONSONANTS: cent, cider, cycle; c̄horus, c̄hute; ġem; light and though (silent), ghost; iñk; elephant; toeṣ, them; speçial, meaṣure, nation, naṭure.

SEE THE FULL KEY ON PAGE 186.

Clē·ȯ·pa′trȧ *n*. The last of the line of Ptolemy kings and queens of Egypt.

clog *n*. A wooden shoe.

clus′ter *n*. A bunch; a group.

cob′ble·stone *n*. A round, flat stone once used for paving streets.

Cōl′ches·tẽr *n*. A town in northeastern England that was burned by Boadicea's warriors.

Cȯl·lō′dï, Cär′lō *n*. An Italian author of children's books, including *The Adventures of Pinocchio*. His real name is Carlo Lorenzini.

cȯm·plaint′ *n*. A statement that something is wrong; a grumbling.

com′pound *n*. A substance formed by two or more elements.

con′cert *n*. A musical performance.

concerto (cȯn·chĕr′tō) *n*. A composition for one or more musical instruments to be played with an orchestra.

conqueror (coñ′ker·ȯr) *n*. One who overcomes an enemy by force.

con′tent *n*. All that is within.

cȯn·vēn′ïent *adj*. Handy; easily reached.

Cȯ·per′ni·cus, Nĭc·ō·lā′us *n*. A Polish astronomer who said that Earth spins and that all the planets circle the sun.

cor·rė·spond′ėnt *n*. A person employed by a magazine, newspaper, or the like to gather news and sometimes take pictures.

coŭn′try *n*. A land; a nation.

cow′ȧrd *n*. A person without courage; a timid, fearful person.

crēak *v*. To make a sharp, harsh noise.

crea′ṭure *n*. A living, moving being, as a person or animal.

Crēte *n*. An island south of Greece in the Mediterranean Sea.

Crī·mē′ȧ *n*. A state in the southwestern part of the Soviet Union.

crim′sọn *adj*. Deep red in color.

crip′pling *adj*. Disabling.

crôss′bōw *n*. A weapon that fires short arrows.

crunch *v*. To make a grinding noise, especially underfoot.

Crụ′sōe, Rob′in·sọn *n*. In the novel by Daniel Defoe, a shipwrecked English sailor.

cupboard (cub′ẽrd) *n*. A cabinet with shelves on which dishes or food is kept.

Curie, Irène (ē·ren′ cū′rïe) *n*. The daughter of Pierre and Marie Curie. She won the Nobel chemistry prize in 1935 with her husband, Frédéric Joliot-Curie, for their work with new radioactive elements.

Cū′rïe, Mȧ·rïe′ *n*. A Polish chemist who won the Nobel physics prize in 1903 with her husband for their work on radiation. She also won the Nobel chemistry prize in 1911 for the discovery of radium and polonium.

Curie, Pierre (pē·âr′ cū′rïe) *n*. A French chemist who won the Nobel physics prize in 1903 with his wife for their work on radiation.

curse *v*. To utter wishes that evil happen to a person or thing; to swear.

Daĕd′·å·lŭs *n*. A legendary architect and sculptor who built the Cretan labyrinth.

deer′mice *n*. White-footed and white-bellied mice of the North American woodlands.

dė·ter′mǐned *adj*. Resolved; decided.

dī′å·ry *n*. A daily record; a journal.

Dip′per *n*. A group of stars in the shape of a ladle or dipper; the Big or Little Dipper.

dĭs·eased′ *adj*. Sick; not healthy; unwell.

dĭs·guīse′ *n*. A costume that changes one's appearance.

Do·lō′rės *n*. A village in central Mexico where Father Hidalgo began the Mexican Revolution.

Doña (dô′nyä) A Spanish title of respect used before a married woman's first name.

down′y *adj*. Like fine hair or feathers.

drĕad *v*. To fear greatly.

drōll *adj*. Humorous in an odd way.

dun′geȯn *n*. A cold, dark, wet underground prison.

dwạrf *n*. A short, stocky person with magical powers.

Ea′gle *n*. The name of the lunar module of the Apollo 11 spacecraft.

ėar′nėst·ly *adv*. Seriously; determinedly.

Ėarth *n*. The third planet from the sun in our solar system. —**ėarth** *n*. The planet on which we live.

ebb *n*. The flow of water back out to sea.

eb′ȯn·y *n*. A black, heavy, long-lasting wood.

Ē′ġўpt *n*. Formerly a kingdom, now a republic, in northeastern Africa.

Ė·lec′tȯr *n*. Any of the German princes that helped elect the emperor of the Holy Roman Empire.

el′ė·mėnt *n*. A substance that cannot be separated into other substances by chemistry.

em′per·ȯr *n*. The ruler of an empire.

en·dụre′ *v*. To bear; to put up with; to hold out.

Ėñg′lånd *n*. A country on the island of Great Britain, just west of Europe.

enough (ė·nȯuf′) *adj*. Sufficient; ample.

en·ter·tain′ *v*. To amuse; to keep occupied.

en·vī′rȯn·mėnt *n*. The surrounding things and conditions.

Pronunciation Key

VOWELS: sat, hăve, āble, fäther, ạll, câre, ȧlone; yet, brĕad, mē, loadėd; ĭt, practĭce, pīlot, machĭne; hot, nō, ôff, wagȯn; fo͝ot, fo͞od; oil, toy; count, town; up, ūse, trụth, pụll; mўth, baby, crў, zephўr.

CONSONANTS: cent, cider, cycle; c̄horus, c̣hute; ġem; light and though (silent), ghost; iñk; elephant; toeṣ, t̲hem; speçial, meaṣure, natıon, naṭure.

SEE THE FULL KEY ON PAGE 186.

191

en′vy *n.* Jealousy.

ė·ter′nȧl *adj.* Lasting forever; endless.

Eū′rȯpe *n.* The second-smallest continent.

ėx·pen′sĭve *adj.* Costing much; valuable.

ėx·pose′ *v.* To uncover; to make open to attack.

fac′tȯ·ry *n.* A building in which goods are made.

fạlse′hŏŏd *n.* An untruth.

fash′iȯn *v.* To make; to shape.

fash′iȯn·ȧ·bly *adv.* In a style popular at the moment.

fīer′y *adj.* Flaming; burning.

fled *v.* To have run away.

flock *n.* A Christian congregation.

fōō-fōō *n.* A hot African dish.

fōre·see′ *v.* To look ahead; to anticipate; to predict.

fȯr·gĭve′ *v.* To pardon; to excuse; to let off.

fȯr′mū·lȧ *n.* A mixture of milk and other ingredients for feeding a baby.

fraġ·īle *adj.* Easily broken; breakable.

French *n.* The language of France.

fum′ble *v.* To handle in a clumsy way; to bungle.

fuñ′gus *n.* A group of spongy plants, including mushrooms and molds, that live on other plants.

fur′nȧce *n.* A large oven used to melt metals.

Gal′i·lē·ō *n.* An Italian astronomer and physicist, the first to use a telescope to study the heavens. His full name was Galileo Galilei.

gal′lȯp *n.* The fastest pace of a horse; a fast run.

Gautier, Felisa Rincón de (fe·lĭ′sa riñ·cōn′ dā go·tyār′) *n.* The mayor of San Juan, Puerto Rico, from 1946 to 1968.

Gautier, Jenaro (hā·nä′ro go·tyār′) *n.* The husband of Felisa Rincón de Gautier.

ġen·er·ā′tiȯn *n.* All the people born at about the same time.

Ġer′mȧn *n.* The language of Germany, Austria, Luxembourg, Liechtenstein, and parts of Switzerland.

Ghana (gä′nȧ) *n.* A country in western Africa.

ghōst′like *adj.* White and like a spirit.

ġin′ġer *n.* The hot, spicy root of the ginger plant, used in cooking.

glee *n.* Merriment; joy.

glisten (glĭs′ėn) *v.* To gleam; to glitter.

gnaw (naw) *v.* To grind on with the teeth.

god *n.* A male object of worship; a male idol.

god′dėss *n.* A female object of worship; a female idol.

Gȯ·lī′ȧth *n.* A giant, leader of the Philistines, who was killed by David with a sling and stone.

Greece *n.* A kingdom in southern Europe, on the Mediterranean Sea.

greed′y *adj.* Unsatisfied; always wanting more.

grim *adj.* Stern; foreboding.

groan *v.* To moan; to make a complaining sound. —*n.* A moan; a complaining sound.

grub *n.* A newly hatched insect; a maggot.

gŭest *n.* A visitor in one's home.

Gutenberg, Johann (yō′hänn gụ̄′tĕn·berg) *n.* The German inventor of movable type for printing.

här′nĕss *n.* The leather straps and metal pieces used to fasten an animal to a plow or carriage.

haugh′ty *adj.* Full of pride; arrogant; snobbish.

hay′lôft *n.* The upper part of a stable or barn where hay is kept.

heärt′wŏŏd *n.* The hard, nonliving wood at the center of a tree trunk.

hĕav′ĕn·ly bŏd′y *n.* A star, planet, moon, or so on in the sky.

Hi·däl′gō, Mĭ·guĕl′ *n.* A Mexican priest and patriot who began the revolt of Mexico against Spain.

Hon·ȯ·lụ̄′lụ̄ *n.* The capital of the state of Hawaii.

hos′pi·tȧl *n.* A building for the care of the sick.

hushed *adj.* Quiet; silent.

Ic′ȧ·rus *n.* The son of Daedalus.

Ĭ·cē′nī *n.* A tribe of Celts who lived in England at the time of Nero.

im·pres′sĭve *adj.* Wonderful; striking; admirable.

improvement (im·prụ̄v′mėnt) *n.* A change for the better.

im′pū·dėnt *adj.* Disrespectful; rude.

In′dĭ·a rub′ber *n.* A springy rubber used to make bouncy balls.

in·dus′trĭ·ȧl *adj.* Having to do with manufacturing and other such businesses.

in′fi·nĭte *adj.* Limitless; immense.

in·jus′tĭce *n.* A wrong; an unfairness.

in′sult *n.* A scornful or disrespectful comment.

island (ī′lȧnd) *n.* A piece of land surrounded by water.

Israel (is′rē·ėl) *n.* The land of the ancient Hebrews at the southeastern end of the Mediterranean Sea, now a modern country formed as a Jewish state by the United Nations.

Israelites (is′rē·ėl·ites) *n.* The people of ancient Israel.

jag'gėd *adj.* Rough edged; notched.

jăve·lin *n.* A light spear used for throwing.

jerk *n.* A short, sharp movement; a twitch.

jȯur'nēy *n.* A trip; a voyage.

judġ'mėnt *n.* A decision in a case of law.

Jụ̄'pi·ter *n.* The largest planet in our solar system, with thirteen or more moons and a small ring.

knelt *v.* To have rested or fallen on bent knees.

lab'ẏ·rinth *n.* A maze; a place with many winding turns.

language (laṅ'gwȧġe) *n.* The speech of a person, nation, or race.

lär'der *n.* A place where food is stored; a pantry.

latch *v.* To fasten with a catch.

lī'ȧr *n.* One who tells falsehoods.

Lit'tle Beâr *n.* Another name for the group of stars known as the Little Dipper.

loam *n.* A fertile soil.

Lȯn'dȯn *n.* A city in southeastern England and the capital of the British Commonwealth.

lum'ber *n.* Sawed timber.

lus'ter *n.* A bright shine on a surface.

mȧ·hog'ȧ·ny *n.* A tropical tree with hard, reddish brown wood.

man·kīnd' *n.* The human race; humanity.

manned space'craft *n.* A spacecraft that is controlled by the people who occupy it.

man'ū·script *n.* A book or paper written by hand.

Marín, Luis Muñoz (lu·is' mū·nyôs' mä·rïn') *n.* The first governor of Puerto Rico to be elected by the people.

mȧ·rïne' *adj.* Having to do with the ocean.

Marine Biological Laboratory (mȧ·rïne' bī·o·loġ'i·cȧl lab'rȧ·tō·ry) *n.* A center for research and study at Woods Hole, Massachusetts.

Märk An'tȯ·ny *n.* A Roman general who hoped to succeed to Julius Caesar's position.

mär'kėt place *n.* An open place in a town where people gather to buy, sell, and trade goods.

Märs *n.* The planet in our solar system fourth-closest to the sun.

Marseilles (mär·say') *n.* A city in southern France; France's largest seaport.

märsh *n.* A swamp; a bog.

mĕad'ōw *n.* An open grassland, especially one used as a hay field.

mĕaṣ'ȗre *v.* To find the size or amount of something.

Mer'cūr·y *n.* The smallest planet in our solar system and the hottest and closest to the sun.

mer'maid *n.* A creature that is half woman and half fish.

Mex'i·cō *n.* A country in North America, just south of the United States.

mid′day *n.* Noon.

Milk′y Way *n.* The name of our galaxy; the group of stars whose light looks like a pathway of milk.

mil′ler *n.* An owner of or worker in a grain mill.

mine *v.* To dig in the earth for metals, jewels, and so on.

Mī′nòs *n.* In Greek mythology, the king of Crete and son of Zeus and Europa.

Min′ò·taur *n.* The monster, half man and half bull, kept in the labyrinth built by Daedalus.

Mi·ñu′ An African word meaning "I do not understand."

mis·un·der·stand′ *v.* To misinterpret; to understand wrongly.

mock *v.* To make fun of.

Mont·gòm′er·y *n.* The capital of the state of Alabama.

mōon *n.* The large natural satellite of the earth.

mōon rock *n.* A rock brought to Earth from the surface of the moon.

Mos′cow *n.* The capital of the Soviet Union.

mot′tō *n.* A wise saying.

mount *v.* To get onto a horse or cycle.

mōurn *v.* To grieve; to be sorry about.

mōurn′er *n.* A person who feels or shows sadness, as at someone's death.

movable type (mụv′à·ble tȳpe) *n.* Pieces of metal or wood used to print words directly onto paper.

movement (mụv′mėnt) *n.* Motion.

mōw′er *n.* One who cuts grass to make hay.

mug *n.* A cup, usually with a handle and made of a heavy material.

mul′bĕr·ry *n.* A tree on whose leaves silkworms feed.

mū·ṣi′ciàn *n.* A person who plays musical instruments.

naugh′ti·nėss *n.* Bad behavior; troublesomeness; mischievousness.

neighborhood (nā′bòr·hŏod) *n.* A part of a town.

neighboring (nā′bòr·ing) *adj.* Near to; adjoining.

Nep′tụne *n.* The planet that is eighth from the sun.

Nile Rĭv′er *n.* The longest river on earth and a center of civilization at the time of Cleopatra.

Nō·bel′ Prize *n.* An annual international award given in chemistry, physics, medicine, literature, and for promoting peace.

Pronunciation Key

VOWELS: sat, hăve, āble, fäther, ạll, câre, ȧlone; yet, brĕad, mē, loadėd; ĭt, practĭce, pīlot, machïne; hot, nō, ôff, wagòn; fŏot, fōod; oil, toy; count, town; up, ūse, trụth, pụll; mȳth, baby, crȳ, zephẏr.

CONSONANTS: **c**ent, **c**ider, **c**ycle; **ch**orus, **ch**ute; **ġ**em; li**gh**t and thou**gh** (silent), **gh**ost; i**ñk**; ele**ph**ant; toe**s**, **th**em; spe**ci**al, mea**ṣ**ure, na**t**ion, na**ṭ**ure.

SEE THE FULL KEY ON PAGE 186.

non·vī′o·lence   *n.* Purposely not using fighting in making a protest.

North Pole   *n.* The northern end of the earth's axis.

nour′ish·ing   *adj.* Sustaining; strengthening; wholesome.

numb   *adj.* Dulled; without feeling.

nurse   *n.* One trained to take care of the sick.

nymph   *n.* A sea, wood, or water goddess.

Oc·tā′vi·an   *n.* The adopted son of Julius Ceasar who became the ruler and first emperor of Rome after Caesar's murder.

ogre (ō′ger)   *n.* A man-eating giant; a monster.

ō′pen house   *n.* An informal meeting in one's home with visitors coming and going as they will.

op·er·ā′tion   *n.* Surgery.

op·por·tū′ni·ty   *n.* A good chance; a favorable time.

or′bit   *v.* To circle a heavenly body, as in a spacecraft.

or′ches·tra   *n.* A group of musicians that plays in concerts, operas, plays or at dances.

ore   *n.* Rock, sand, or dirt that contains a mineral.

out′cast   *n.* An exile; a vagabond.

out′skirts   *n.* The outer parts of a city or town.

pace   *n.* A step; a stride.

page   *n.* A boy attendant.

pale   *adj.* Light in color.

pär′tridge   *n.* A wild bird related to the chicken.

pas′sage·way   *n.* A hall; a corridor.

Paulinus, Suetonius (swi·tō′ni·us pau·lī′nus)   *n.* The Roman general who was governor of Britain at the time of Nero.

peas′ant   *n.* A poor country person; a poor farm worker.

Phil′ip II   *n.* In ancient Greece, the father of Alexander III.

Phi′lis·tines   *n.* A people of the ancient Middle East who often had wars with Israel.

Phoe·ni′cians   *n.* An ancient tribe of people who lived on the eastern shore of the Mediterranean Sea and were sailors and traders.

phō·tō·jour′nal·ism   *n.* A way of reporting news by using mostly pictures.

phys′ics   *n.* The science that deals with natural forces.

plain   *n.* A stretch of flat country; a prairie.

plan′et   *n.* Any of the nine heavenly bodies, including Earth, that revolve around the sun and shine by reflecting its light.

plun′der   *v.* To rob; to take goods or valuables by force.

Plū′tō   *n.* The planet that is ninth from the sun.

po·lit′i·cal pär′ty   *n.* A group of people with similar political goals who work together to increase their strength in the government.

pop·ū·lā′tion *n.* All the people in one area or group.

pov′er·ty *n.* Need or want.

pow′er *n.* Strength; control; mastery.

pranc′ing *adj.* Springing; jumping around.

prē′cious *adj.* Costly; loved; prized.

prïest *n.* A person whose job is to perform religious rites.

print′ing press *n.* A machine for printing from inked type, plates, and so on.

pris′on *n.* A place where those accused of or sentenced for a crime must stay; a jail.

prò·ces′sion *n.* A group of people marching in line; a parade.

prop′er *adj.* Right; correct; suitable.

prop′er·ly *adv.* Rightly; correctly; suitably.

Prot′ès·tànt *adj.* Of or belonging to the Christian churches that broke away from the Roman Catholic church.

Ptolemies (tol′é·mēs) *n.* A line of kings and queens of Egypt, ending with Cleopatra.

pub′lic *n.* The people; the community.

Puerto Rico (pwĕr′tò rï′cō) *n.* An island in the West Indies that is self-governing but is protected by the United States.

pup′pet *n.* A doll controlled by strings or by hand.

puz′zle *v.* To confuse; to perplex.

quar·tet′ *n.* A musical composition for four persons or instruments.

rā′cial *n.* Of or concerning a group of people with the same inherited physical traits, such as color of skin or shape of body.

rack *n.* A frame for holding or drying articles.

rā·dï·ō·ac′tïve *adj.* Giving off energy as rays or particles.

rā′dï·um *n.* A metal that is very radioactive.

raf′ter *n.* A roof beam.

rage *n.* Anger; passion; fury.

rap *v.* To strike a sharp blow.

rēap′er *n.* A person who cuts grain.

rēar *v.* In animals, to rise on the hind legs.

rē·birth′ *n.* A renewal; a revival.

reef. *n.* A ridge of coral, sand, or rocks near the surface of the sea.

rė·form′ *n.* An improvement; a change for the better.

rė·fūṣe′ *v.* To decline; to reject; to say no to.

rė·lā′tiȯn *n.* A relative.

rė·märk′å·ble *adj.* Unusual; extraordinary; worth noticing.

rep′tĭle *n.* A group of cold-blooded animals with scales that creep or crawl, including snakes and lizards.

rest′lėss *adj.* Unable to rest, be quiet, or relax.

Rō′mȧn *n.* Of or belonging to Rome.

Rome *n.* The capital of the Roman Empire at the time of Julius Caesar; now the capital of Italy.

rud′der *n.* The part of a ship or airplane by which it is steered.

rụle *v.* To govern; to control.

rụ′rȧl *adj.* Having to do with the countryside.

Rus′ṣià *n.* A country in northern Europe and Asia.

saġe *n.* A wise man; a philosopher.

sạlt′cel·lȧr *n.* A small dish or shaker for salt.

San Juan (san wän) *n.* The capital of Puerto Rico.

Sat′urn *n.* The large planet sixth from the sun, noted for its system of rings.

sav′aġe *n.* An uncivilized person; a barbarian.

Scot′lånd *n.* A country in northern Great Britain.

Scots *n.* The people of Scotland.

scuf′fling *adj.* With noises made by moving the feet quickly back and forth.

scur′vy *adj.* Bad; worthless.

Scụ′tä·rï *n.* The old name for the town of Uskudar, Turkey, where Florence Nightingale had her hospital.

sen′try *n.* A soldier on guard duty.

shelf fuñ′gus *n.* A mushroomlike fungus that grows on trees in the shape of brackets.

shel′ter *n.* Something that protects; cover.

shepherd (shep′ėrd) *n.* One who takes care of sheep.

shore *n.* The land near a large body of water; the coast.

shȯv′ėl *n.* A broad-bladed spade for lifting loose dirt.

shrïek *n.* A shout; a yell.

sĭeve *n.* A mesh-bottomed container for separating fine from coarse matter or for draining; a sifter.

sigh *n.* A long, loud breathing out.

silk′wȯrm *n.* The larva of a moth that spins a silk cocoon.

sip *v.* To drink in small mouthfuls; to taste.

skip′per *n.* A boat captain or master.

slen′der·er *adj.* Slimmer; slighter.

sling *n.* A strap used for hurling rocks.

smȯṯh′er *v.* To suffocate; to choke.

Sol′ȯ·mȯn *n.* The king of Israel from 973 to 933 B.C.

South Å·mĕr′i·cå *n.* The fourth-largest continent.

Sō′vǐ·et *adj*. Of or from the Soviet Union, or Russia.

Span′ish *n*. The language of Spain and many countries in Latin America.

spâre *v*. To avoid punishing or hurting someone.

splen′dȯr *n*. Grandness; magnificence.

spray *n*. Fine particles of a liquid.

stale *adj*. Dull and uninteresting.

stär′tle *v*. To frighten; to surprise; to astonish.

stout′nėss *n*. Fatness; plumpness.

stu̧′dǐ·ō *n*. An artist's or photographer's workroom.

sul′phur *n*. A yellow mineral with a sharp odor; brimstone.

sun *n*. The star at the center of our solar system that provides heat and light for the earth.

sway *v*. To move from side to side; to swing.

sweep *n*. A long, curving motion.

Switzerland (swit′ser·lȧnd) *n*. A mountainous country in central Europe.

sword (sōrd) *n*. A long, narrow-bladed weapon.

sy̆m′phȯ·ny *n*. A musical composition to be played by an orchestra.

tel′ė·scope *n*. An instrument that makes distant objects seem near.

tend *v*. To care for; to watch over.

ter′mite *n*. A white, antlike creature that eats wood.

thatched roof *n*. A roof covered with straw or similar material.

thō′rǐ·um *n*. A grayish metal that is radioactive.

thōugh *adv*. However.

thump *v*. To strike with a heavy, blunt instrument or the fist.

'tis A contraction of *it is*.

tor·pē′dō *v*. To hit with an exploding shell that travels underwater.

tow′el-horse *n*. A towel rack.

trade′märk *n*. A name or symbol that identifies someone or something.

traġ′ė·dy *n*. A disaster.

Tran·quǐl′i·ty Base *n*. The place on the Sea of Tranquility on the moon where the Apollo 11 spacecraft landed.

trot *n*. A slow run.

trudge *v*. To walk wearily and heavily; to plod.

twit′ter *v*. To make a series of high, sharp, light sounds like a bird's chirp.

ty̆′rȧnt *n*. A cruel and severe ruler.

Pronunciation Key

VOWELS: sat, hă̆ve, āble, fäther, ạll, câre, ȧlone; yet, brĕad, mē, loadėd; it, practĭce, pī̆lot, machī̆ne; hot, nō, ôff, wagȯn; fo͝ot, fo͞od; oil, toy; count, town; up, ūse, tru̧th, pu̧ll; my̆th, baby, cry̆, zephy̆r.

CONSONANTS: **c**ent, **c**ider, **c**y**c**le; **c̄**horus, **c̆**hute; ġem; light and thoug**h** (silent), g**h**ost; iñk; ele**ph**ant; toe**s̠**, **t̠h**em; spe**c**ial, mea**s̠**ure, na**t**ion, na**t̠**ure.

SEE THE FULL KEY ON PAGE 186.

un·grate′fŭl *adj*. Unthankful; not showing appreciation.

un·latch′ *v*. To open; to unfasten.

un·wrapped′ *adj*. Undone; opened.

up′rīs·ing *n*. A revolt; a revolution.

ū·rā′nĭ·um *n*. A heavy, hard, white radioactive metal.

Ūr′ȧ·nus *n*. A large planet that lies seventh from the sun in our solar system.

val′ūe *n*. The worth of an object.

Vē′nus *n*. The planet in our solar system that is second-closest to the sun, often called the morning or evening star.

Verulamium (vĕr·yu̧·lā′mĭ·um) *n*. The old Roman name for a town in southeastern England, now called St. Albans.

vic′tȯ·ry *n*. The defeat of an enemy in battle; a conquest; a triumph.

Vĭ·en′nȧ *n*. The capital of Austria, on the Danube River.

vī·ō′lȧ *n*. A stringed musical instrument similar to a violin but a little larger and with a deeper tone.

vī·ȯ·lin′ *n*. A stringed musical instrument played with a bow; a fiddle.

Virgin of Guadalupe (vir′g̣in of gwä·dȧ·lu̧pe′) *n*. The patron saint of Mexico.

vĭ′şiȯn *n*. A dream.

Vĭ′vȧ The Spanish word meaning ''long live.''

wea′ry *adj*. Exhausted; fatigued; tired.

wid′ōwed *adj*. Having had one's husband die.

wis′dȯm *n*. The ability to use knowledge; sense.

with′er *v*. To fade; to perish.

wou̧nd *v*. To injure; to harm.

yam *n*. A vegetable similar to the sweet potato.